Semantic Relationism

The Blackwell/Brown Lectures in Philosophy

Series Editor: Ernest Sosa, Brown University

The Blackwell/Brown Lectures in Philosophy present compact books distilling cutting-edge research from across the discipline. Based on public lectures presented at Brown University, the books in the series are by established scholars of the highest caliber, presenting their work in a clear and concise format.

1. *Semantic Relationism* by Kit Fine
2. *The Philosophy of Philosophy* by Timothy Williamson

Forthcoming books by Frank Jackson, Philip Pettit, and John Broome

Semantic Relationism

Kit Fine

WILEY-BLACKWELL

A John Wiley & Sons, Ltd., Publication

This paperback edition first published 2009
© 2009 Kit Fine
Edition history: Blackwell Publishing Ltd (hardback, 2007)

Blackwell Publishing was acquired by John Wiley & Sons in February 2007. Blackwell's publishing program has been merged with Wiley's global Scientific, Technical, and Medical business to form Wiley-Blackwell.

Registered Office
John Wiley & Sons Ltd, The Atrium, Southern Gate, Chichester, West Sussex, PO19 8SQ, United Kingdom

Editorial Offices
350 Main Street, Malden, MA 02148-5020, USA
9600 Garsington Road, Oxford, OX4 2DQ, UK
The Atrium, Southern Gate, Chichester, West Sussex, PO19 8SQ, UK

For details of our global editorial offices, for customer services, and for information about how to apply for permission to reuse the copyright material in this book please see our website at www.wiley.com/wiley-blackwell.

Library of Congress Cataloging-in-Publication Data

Fine, Kit.
Semantic relationism / Kit Fine.
    p. cm. — (The Blackwell/Brown lectures in philosophy)
Includes bibliographical references and index.
ISBN-13: 978-1-4051-0843-0 (hardcover : alk. paper)   ISBN-13: 978-1-4051-9669-7 (paperback: alk. paper)
1. Semantics.   2. Semantics (Philosophy)   I. Title.
P325.F53 2007
401.43—dc22
2007003774

A catalogue record for this book is available from the British Library.

Set in 10.5 on 13 pt Sabon by SNP Best-set Typesetter Ltd., Hong Kong
Printed and bound in Singapore

01   2009

Contents

Preface

The ideas behind these lectures had their origin in the early 1980s. There was then a great deal of excitement over the "new" theory of direct reference, but many of those who were attracted to the theory were also worried about the challenge posed by Frege's puzzle. How could they claim, as the theory seemed to require, that the meaning of "Cicero = Tully" was the same as "Cicero = Cicero," when the one was plainly informative and the other not?

I myself faced a similar problem over the role of variables. I had previously attempted to develop a theory of variable or arbitrary objects. According to this theory, a variable should be taken to signify a variable object, something which we might loosely identify with the variable's meaning or abstract role. However, even though the variables x and y, when considered on their own, should be taken to signify the same variable object, they should not be taken to signify the same variable object when considered together, since otherwise we would lose the relevant distinction between $x = y$ and $x = x$. It seemed clear to me that the two problems were essentially the same and that there should be a common solution to them both, even though it was not then clear to me what the solution should be.

I worried about this issue on and off for the next 15 years until it dawned on me that it could only be adequately solved by making a fundamental break with semantics as it is usually conceived. One must take account of the meaning that expressions have, not only when considered on their own but also when they are considered together; the meaning relation between them is not simply to be regarded as a product of their individual meanings. Once we embrace this liberating thought, we can then see how the usual referential view of the meaning of variables and names can be retained and yet the difficulties over Frege-type puzzles avoided.

It was, therefore, opportune when Ernie Sosa asked me to give the first Blackwell/Brown lecture for the Fall of 2002, since this provided me with an opportunity to develop these ideas, which were still in a very inchoate form, and to discuss them with a wonderful group of philosophers. I have since presented the material on a variety of other occasions: as the John Locke Lectures for Trinity Term of 2003; at two seminars in philosophy at NYU during the Spring of 2002 and the Fall of 2004; and in a number of talks within Europe and the USA. I am extremely grateful to the participants at these meetings and, in particular, to Joseph Almog, Tony Anderson, George Bealer, Justin Broakes, Ray Buchanan, Tyler Burge, John Campbell, Ruth Chang, Paul Coppock, David Corfield, Louis Derosset, Cian Dorr, Michael Dummett, Hartry Field, Paul Hovda, Carrie Jenkins, David Kaplan, Jaegwon Kim, Saul Kripke, Robert May, Friederike Moltmann, Sarah Moss, Angel Pinillos, Nathan Salmon, Marco Santambrogio, Joshua Schecter, Stephen Schiffer, Scott Soames, Seunghyun Song, Ernest Sosa, Bas van Fraassen, Brian Weatherstone, Tim Williamson, and Crispin Wright. I am also grateful to two anonymous referees who provided me with many valuable comments. Even if meaning is not relational, as I have supposed, the present contribution to philosophy certainly is.

The present book is loosely based upon the lectures I gave at Brown and I have tried to keep to something like the original lecture format. This has meant that a number of topics have not been pursued, though I have given a brief account of some of the more important of these topics in the final chapter. It has also meant that scholarly allusions have been kept to a minimum. I have, in particular, made no attempt to compare my own work with the loosely related work of Almog (2006), Fiengo and May (2005), Lawlor (2005), and Lieb (1983). This is a "bare-bones" account, simply intended to convey the essential ideas; and I hope later to provide a fuller account that is both broader in its scope and much more thorough in its treatment of particular topics.

Introduction

Many philosophers and linguists have remarked on the great expressive capacity of language – its capacity, on the basis of a finite vocabulary and a finite stock of syntactic rules, to express an infinitude of different thoughts. But equally remarkable, though less rarely remarked, is a capacity in the opposite direction – a capacity not to express different thoughts, but the very same thought from one occasion to the next. I say "Cicero is an orator"; I then repeat "Cicero is an orator"; you say "Cicero is an orator"; you then repeat "Cicero is an orator"; and so on. Although we produce a multitude of different utterances, we all somehow manage to say the same thing. But how?

Perhaps the reason this contrasting capacity has gone relatively unremarked is that it is not taken to be remarkable. After all, if I have said something once, then what is the point in saying it again? But such a response could not be more off the mark. Just imagine that for some reason we were not able to say the same thing from one occasion of use to another. Reasoning would then be at a stand still. To take a simple illustration, the validity of modus ponens – the inference from sentences of the form "S" and "if S then T" to the sentence "T" – depends upon the two uses of S and the two uses of T being used to say the same thing. Communication, or the transmission of information, would also be impossible. I may attempt to inform you in the words "Cicero is an orator" that Cicero is an orator. But how can you can pass this information on, or even report what I said, if you are unable to say what I said? And if we allow that it might not be possible to *think* the same thought from one occasion to the next, then the consequences become even more devastating. Memory, for example, would become impossible since it depends upon remembering the content of what I had previously remembered or thought.

There is another reason the contrasting capacity might have gone unremarked. For it might have been thought to be evident in what it consists. If it is asked what kind of same-saying is involved in inference or communication, then it is simply this: I say one thing on one occasion and I or you say the same thing on another occasion. The relevant form of same-saying is simply a matter of saying the *same thing*.

This obvious account of the capacity might be called the "resemblance view," since it takes same-saying to consist in a resemblance in what is said. Now there is a way in which the resemblance view might be truistic. If you and I say the same thing, then our utterances must have something in common. For my utterance says the same as my utterance and your utterance also says the same as my utterance. They, therefore, have in common that each says the same as my utterance.

However, this kind of resemblance is completely uninteresting. If the resemblance view is to have any interest or "bite," then it should presumably be based upon the idea that the two utterances have some *intrinsic* semantic features in common, ones that are not a matter of their semantic relationship to other expressions, and that it is this which accounts for their saying the same thing. Two identical twins look alike; and they look alike in virtue of sharing some intrinsic physical features (the same crooked nose etc.). It must be supposed that this is how it is with the utterances; they are semantic twins, as it were, that bear the relevant semantic features "on their face." We might put it this way. Suppose we were to take a "semantic snapshot" of my utterance, one that reveals its semantic features without regard to its semantic relationship to other utterances. Suppose we were also to take a semantic snapshot of your utterance. The view is that it can then be determined on the basis of these semantic snapshots whether or not the two utterances say the same thing. Or to state the view more generally, it will be maintained that, once we have semantic snapshots for all of the meaningful utterances or expressions of a language, then nothing more need be said about how the meaning of one utterance or expression might relate to the meaning of another, since this will already be determined by their meaning what they do.

The resemblance view is very attractive and it has been implicitly presupposed by the major approaches to the theory of meaning. Of course, part of what might make the view seem so attractive is the easy slide from the truistic version of the resemblance view to the more substantive version. But far more significant is the fact that it is hard to see either why an alternative is necessary or what it might be. Two utterances that say the same thing clearly do have some common intrinsic semantic features; and it is not at all clear either why these are not sufficient to guarantee that they say the same thing or, if they do not, what the additional factors that guarantee that they do might be.

All the same, I wish to argue that the view is mistaken – and deeply mistaken at that. What I would like to propose in its place is a relational view of meaning. According to this view – which I call "Semantic Relationism" – the fact that two utterances say the same thing is not entirely a matter of their intrinsic semantic features; it may also turn on semantic relationships among the utterances or their parts which are not reducible to those features. We must, therefore, recognize that there may be *irreducible* semantic relationships, ones not reducible to the intrinsic semantic features of the expressions between which they hold. Thus even if we were to take a semantic snapshot of each expression in our language, one that completely displays its intrinsic semantic features, it might not be evident from these snapshots what semantic relationships among the expressions should hold. The picture of an assemblage of semantic snapshots must be supplemented by a picture in which these snapshots are connected, one to the other, by semantic threads. This snapshot goes with this one in this way, that snapshot with that one in that way, yet there is no determining from the snapshots themselves how the semantic threads between them should go. And what goes for language also goes for thought; there is no determining the full content of what someone thinks or believes from the individual things that he thinks or believes; we must also look at the threads that tie the contents of these thoughts or beliefs together.

It is important, if the present doctrine of semantic relationism is to be properly understood, that it be distinguished from the more familiar doctrine of semantic holism. The underlying dispute between the holists and their opponents is over the proper form of semantic theory. For the holists, a proper theory will be broadly inferential in character – it will deal with the inferential relationships among different expressions or with other aspects of their inferential or conceptual role – while, for their opponents, it will be representational in character – it will attempt to describe the relationship between the expressions of the language and the reality it is meant to represent. But both sides to the dispute will agree that if a representational semantics is adopted then it should be atomistic in form while if an inferential semantics is adopted it should be holistic in form.

It is, however, on this point of agreement that I wish to focus the current dispute. Our concern is to reject Atomism for a *representational* form of semantics; and so our disagreement is as much with the holists as with their opponents. The need for semantic relationships arises, on the present view, not from the desire to account for inferential role but from the desire to account for the straightforwardly representational features of language.

We can better understand what is distinctive about the present position – and also how radical it is – by means of an analogy with the substantivalist conception of space. The substantivalist believes that a fundamental account of the spatial facts should incorporate an assignment of location to each spatial object; and similarly, the representationalist will think that a fundamental account of the semantic facts should incorporate an assignment of meaning, or representational role, to each meaningful expression. Now it would be quite bizarre for the substantivalist to believe that the fundamental spatial facts should also include spatial relationships among the spatial objects. For the natural – almost irresistible – view is that the spatial relationships among objects will be determined by the corresponding spatial relationships among their locations. What is it for two objects to be coincident? It is for their locations to be the same. What is it for two objects to be a foot apart? It is for their locations to be a foot apart. And similarly for other spatial relations. A corresponding view about semantical relationships would appear to be equally plausible for the representationalist. What is it for two expressions to be synonymous? It is for their meaning to be the same. What is it for them to be contraries? It is for their meanings to be contraries. And similarly for other semantical relationships. But it is exactly this analogous view that I wish to reject. Not all semantical relationships among expressions are induced by corresponding relationships among their meanings and even synonymy – which might be thought to be a paradigm of an induced relationship – is not always properly so regarded. It should be recognized that both the intrinsic and the relational features of expressions may be relevant to the representational semantics of any given language.

The principal, though not the only, form of semantic relation is what I call *coordination*. This is the very strongest relation of synonymy or being semantically the same; and the various chapters are loosely organized around how the different forms of coordination might be manifested – whether in the use of variables or names, or in thought, or in the connection between thought and language, or in the connections between different speakers and thinkers. Each form of coordination gives rise to some familiar puzzles – to Russell's antinomy of the variable, to Frege's puzzle in its various guises, and to Kripke's puzzle about belief; and the argument for a relationist position is made by showing how these puzzles can only be adequately solved by adopting relationist ideas. Very roughly, the antinomy of the variable will show that relationism is true of variables, Frege's puzzle that it is true of names, and Kripke's puzzle that is true, though in a much more radical way than one might have imagined, of how the use of names connects up with objects of thought. Thus the book is a sustained attempt to develop a single unified account of these various puzzles. But it is also an attempt to defend a referentialist position within the philosophy of language. For coordination can do much of the work of sense; and by adopting a relationist view of coordination, the referentialist can secure many of the advantages of the Fregean position without being committed to the existence of sense. Thus the book offers the hope that some of the more seemingly intractable problems with the referentialist position can be overcome.

Chapter 1

Coordination among Variables

It is generally supposed – by logicians and philosophers alike – that we now possess a perfectly good understanding of how variables work in the symbolism of logic and mathematics. Once Frege had provided a clear syntactic account of variables and once Tarski had supplemented this with a rigorous semantic account, it would appear that there was nothing more of significance to be said. It seems to me, however, that this common view is mistaken. There are deep problems concerning the role of variables that have never been properly recognized, let alone solved, and once we attempt to solve them we see that they have profound implications not only for our understanding of variables but also for our understanding of other forms of expression and for the general nature of semantics.[1]

It is my aim in the present book to explain what these problems are and how they are to be solved. I begin with an antinomy concerning the role of variables which I believe any satisfactory account should address (section A). I then argue that the three main semantical schemes currently on the market – the Tarskian, the instantial and the algebraic – are unsuccessful in solving the puzzle (sections B and C) or in providing a satisfactory semantics for first-order logic (sections D and E). Finally, I offer an alternative scheme that it is capable of solving the antinomy (section F) and of providing a more satisfactory semantics for first-order logic (section G). It is based upon the new approach to representational semantics, which I previously called "semantic relationism"; and in the following chapters, I discuss the implications of this approach for the semantics of names and belief-reports.

A fair deal of the present chapter is not strictly relevant to the rest of the book and readers whose interests lie more in the philosophy of language than in philosophical logic might wish to restrict their attention to sections A and F before proceeding to the other chapters.

A.   The Antinomy of the Variable

In what follows I shall make free use of the notion of *semantic role*. By this, I do not have in mind some technical notion of the kind that one might find in formal semantics but a non-technical notion whose application may already be taken to be implicit in our understanding of a given language or symbolism. For in any meaningful expression, there is something conventional – having to do with actual symbols or words used – and something nonconventional – having to do with the representational function of those symbols or words. And "semantic role" is just my term for this essentially nonconventional aspect of a meaningful expression.

Suppose that we have two variables, say "x" and "y"; and suppose that they range over the same domain of individuals, say the domain of all real numbers. Then it appears as if we wish to say contradictory things about their semantic role. For when we consider their semantic role in two distinct expressions – such as "$x > 0$" and "$y > 0$," we wish to say that it is the same. Indeed, this would appear to be as clear a case as one could hope to have of a merely "conventional" or "notational" difference; the difference is merely in the choice of the symbol and not at all in linguistic function. On the one hand, when we consider the semantic role of the variables in the same expression – such as in "$x > y$" – then it seems equally clear that it is different. Indeed, it would appear to be essential to the semantic role of the expression as a whole that it contains two distinct variables, not two occurrences of the same variable, and presumably this is because the roles of the distinct variables are not the same.

Generalizing from our example, we arrive at the following two claims:

Semantic Sameness (SS): Any two variables (ranging over a given domain of objects) have the same semantic role; and
Semantic Difference (SD): Any two variables (ranging over a given domain of objects) have a different semantic role.

Yet we cannot univocally maintain both (given that there are indeed two variables over a given domain!).

We might call this puzzle the *antinomy of the variable*.[2] It was first stated by Russell, though in ontological rather than semantical fashion. He writes (1903, section 93): "x is, in some sense, the object denoted by *any term*; yet this can hardly be strictly maintained, for different variables may occur in a proposition, yet the object denoted by *any term*, one would suppose, is unique." It also bears a close affinity with Frege's puzzle concerning names (Frege, 1952), which will be considered in the next two chapters.

Clearly, any resolution of the conflict that accepts both assumptions must begin by locating an ambiguity in the phrase "same semantic role." Whatever the sense in which the variables x and y are semantically the same in "$x > 0$" and "$y > 0$" cannot be the sense in which they fail to be semantically the same in "$x > y$." Now as a first stab towards locating the ambiguity, we might appeal to a notion of context. The variable "x" in the context of the formula "$x > 0$" plays the same semantic role as the variable "y" in the context of the formula "$y > 0$." On the other hand, the two variables x and y will play different semantic roles within the context of the single formula "$x > y$." Thus SS will hold for sameness of semantic role in the *cross*-contextual sense while SD will hold for difference of semantic role in the *intra*-contextual sense; and, given the ambiguity in the respective senses of "same" and "different" role, contradiction is avoided.

Natural as this response may be, it does not really solve the puzzle but merely pushes it back a step. For why do we say that the variables x and y have a different semantic role in "$x > y$?" Clearly, it has to do with the fact that the occurrence of y cannot be replaced by x without a change in overall semantic role; the role of x, y in "$x < y$" is different from the role of x, x in "$x < x$." In other words, the intra-contextual difference in semantic role between the variables x and y within the single formula "$x > y$" amounts to a cross-contextual difference in semantic role between the pair of variables x, y in "$x > y$" and the pair of variables x, x in "$x > x$." And, in general, to say that there is an intra-contextual difference between x and y, in the intended sense, is just to say that there is cross-contextual difference between the pair of variables x, y and the pair x, x.

We may therefore state SS and SD in the following form:

SS' there is no cross-contextual difference in semantic role between
the variables x and y; and

SD' there is a cross-contextual difference in semantic role between
the pair of variables x, y and the pair x, x,

using a univocal notion of semantic role throughout.

In contrast to the earlier formulation, there is now no explicit
contradiction. But there is still a difficulty in seeing how the two
claims, SS' and SD', might both be true. For how can there be a cross-
contextual difference in semantic role between the pair of variables
x, y and the pair x, x unless there is a cross-contextual semantic difference between the variables x and y themselves? What else could
account for the difference in semantic role between the pairs x, y and
x, x except a semantic difference in the individual variables x and y?
Or to put it another way, if there is a semantic difference between
x, y and x, x, then there must be a semantic difference between x and
y; and it is hard to see why this difference should only be "turned
on" or made manifest when the variables are used in the same context
and not when they are used in different contexts.

The puzzle therefore remains; and any solution to the puzzle should
either explain how SS' and SD' might be compatible, notwithstanding
appearances to the contrary, or it must explain how one of SS' or SD'
might reasonably be rejected.

B.   The Tarskian Approach

It might be thought that the solution to our puzzle should be sought
in the various semantics that have been developed for the language
of predicate logic. After all, it is presumably the aim of these semantics to account for the semantic role of the expressions with which
they deal; and so we should expect them to account, in particular,
for the semantic role of variables.

However, when we turn to the various semantics that have in fact
been developed, we find them not entirely suited to the purpose. I shall
consider the three main proposals on the market. There are, of course,
others though I am not aware that they do any better. We begin with
the semantic approach of Tarski (1936). The reader will recall that
the Tarski semantics proceeds by defining a relation of satisfaction

between assignments and formulas. To fix our ideas, let us suppose that the variables of our language are $x_1, x_2, \ldots$ and that the domain of discourse is D. We may take an *assignment* to be a function taking each variable of the language into an individual from D; and the semantics will then specify – by means either of a definition or of a set of axioms – what it is for each kind of formula to be satisfied by an assignment. It will state for example that an assignment satisfies the formula ~B just in case it fails to satisfy B or that an assignment satisfies the formula $\forall x$B just in case every x-variant of the assignment (differing at most on the value assigned to x) satisfies B.

Now what account, within the framework of the Tarski semantics, can be given of the semantic role of the variables? There would appear to be only two options. The first is to take the semantic role of a variable to be given by its range of values (the domain D in the case above). Indeed, quite apart from the connection with the Tarski semantics, this is the usual way of indicating how a variable is to be interpreted: one simply specifies its range of values.

Now this approach does indeed account for the fact that the semantic role of any two variables x and y (with an identical range of values) is the same. But it does nothing to account for the semantic difference between the pairs of variables x, y and x, x; and nor is any reason given for disputing the intuitive difference in semantic role.

The other option is to take the semantic role of a variable to be what one might call its "semantic value" under the given semantics. The semantic values are those entities which are assigned (or which might be taken to be assigned) to the meaningful expressions of the language and with respect to which the semantics for the language is compositional. When we examine the Tarski semantics, we see that the semantic value of an open formula (one containing free variables) may be taken to be the function that takes each assignment into the "truth-value" of the formula under that assignment (the TRUE if the formula is satisfied by the assignment and the FALSE otherwise) and, similarly, the semantic value of an open term might be taken to be the function that takes each assignment into the denotation of the term under that assignment. Thus the semantic value of the formula $x > 0$ (under the natural interpretation of the language) would be the function that takes any assignment into TRUE if the number it assigns to x is positive and into FALSE otherwise; and the semantic value of the term $x + y$ would be the function which takes any assignment into the sum of the numbers which it assigns to x and y. We then easily see that the Tarski semantics is compositional with respect to the semantic values as so conceived; it "computes" the semantic value of a complex expression on the basis of the semantic values of the simpler expressions from which it is derived.

Under this conception of semantic value, the semantic value of a variable x will be a special case of the semantic value of a term; it will be a function which takes each assignment into the individual which it assigns to x. It is, therefore, clear, if we identify semantic roles and semantic values, that x and y will differ in their semantic roles; for if we take any assignment which assigns different individuals to x and y (this requires, of course, that there be at least two individuals in the domain!), then the semantic value of x will deliver the one individual in application to that assignment while the semantic value of y will deliver the other individual in application to the assignment.

We therefore secure the semantic difference between the pairs x, y and x, x under this account of semantic role. However, we are unable to account for the fact that the semantic role of the variables x and y is the same in the cross-contextual case; and nor is any reason given for disputing the intuitive identity of semantic role in this case. What we have at best is a partial identity of semantic role, in that the range of the two variables is the same. But this is something that holds equally of the cross-contextual and intra-contextual cases.

There is another, perhaps more serious, problem with the approach. For although it posits a difference between the variables x and y (and hence between the pairs x, y and x, x), it does nothing to account for their *semantic* difference. For in the last analysis, the posited difference between the semantic values for x and y simply turns on the difference between the variables x and y themselves. Indeed, we may get from the semantic value for x – that is, the appropriate function from assignments to individuals – to the semantic value for y simply be interchanging the roles of the variables x and y themselves. Thus what we secure on this approach, strictly speaking, is not a *semantic* difference, one lying on the non-conventional side of language, but a *typographic* difference, one lying purely on the conventional side of language; and so we have done nothing to say in what the semantic difference between x and y (or between x, y and x, x) properly consists.

C.   The Rejection of Semantic Role

In stating the antinomy of the variable, we have presupposed that variables *have* a semantic role; and it might be thought that this is the root cause of our difficulties. For it might be thought that our understanding of variables is inseparable from their role in quantification or other forms of variable-binding and that any attempt to explain the role of *free* variables, apart from their connection with the apparatus of binding, must, therefore, fail.

There is a familiar approach to the semantics of predicate logic that might appear to lend some support to this point of view. For in attempting to provide a semantics for quantified sentences, we face a problem that is in some ways analogous to our antinomy. We wish to assign a semantic value to a quantified sentence, such as $\exists x(x > 0)$; and we naturally do this on the basis of the semantic value assigned to the open sentence $x > 0$ that is governed by the quantifier. But, given that $x > 0$ and $y > 0$ are mere notational variants, they should be assigned the same semantic value; and so we should assign the same semantic value to $\exists x(x > 0)$ and $\exists x(y > 0)$ – which is clearly unacceptable.

Now one solution to this problem, though not perhaps the only one, is to deny that the semantic value of $\exists x(x > 0)$ is to be assigned on the basis of the semantic value assigned to $x > 0$; and once this line is adopted, then consistency demands that we never appeal to the semantic value of an open expression in determining the semantic value of a closed expression. In other words, the semantics for closed expressions should be "autonomous" in the sense of never making a detour through the semantics of open expressions.

There are two main ways in which autonomy of this sort might be achieved. We might call them the *instantial* and the *algebraic* approaches respectively. According to the first, the semantic value of a quantified sentence such as $\exists x(x > 0)$ is made to depend upon the semantic value of a closed instance $c > 0$ such as $3 > 0$. The intuitive idea behind this proposal is that, given an understanding of a closed instance $c > 0$, we thereby understand what it is for an arbitrary individual to satisfy the condition of being greater than 0 and are thereby in a position to understand what it is for some individual or other to satisfy this condition.[3]

According to the second approach, the semantic value of a quantified sentence such as $\exists x(x > 0)$ is made, in the first place, to depend upon the semantic value of the corresponding λ-term $\lambda x(x > 0)$, denoting the property of being greater than 0. Of course, this merely pushes the problem back a step, since we now need to account for the semantic value of the λ-terms in question. But this may be done by successively reducing the complexity of the λ-terms. The semantic value of $\lambda x{\sim}(x > 0)$, for example, may be taken to be the "negation" of the semantic value of $\lambda x(x > 0)$, while the semantic value of $\lambda xy(x \leq y \vee y \leq x)$ may be taken to be the "disjunction" of the semantic values of $\lambda xy(x \leq y)$ and $\lambda xy(y \leq x)$. In this way, the λ-bindings may be driven inwards to the atomic formulas of the symbolism and their application to the atomic formulas may then be replaced by the application of various "algebraic" operations to the properties or relations signified by the primitive predicates.[4]

In discussing these proposals, it is important to distinguish between two different questions. The first is whether they are plausible or even viable. Can a semantics of the proposed sort be given that is faithful to the way we actually understand the symbolism? The second question is whether open expressions should be taken to have a semantic role (which it might then be part of the aim of semantics to capture).

Of course, if there is an autonomous semantics for closed expressions, then that deprives us of one reason for thinking that open expressions have a semantic role, since they are not required to have a semantic role in order to account for the semantics of closed expressions; and I suspect that many philosophers who have been attracted to the idea of an autonomous semantics for closed expressions have been inclined, on this basis, to reject a semantic role for open expressions. It seems to me, however, that there are strong independent reasons for thinking that open expressions do indeed have a semantic role.

The intuitive evidence for this appears to be overwhelming. Surely, we are inclined to think, it is at least part of the semantic role of an open term to represent a range of values. It will be part of the semantic role of the term "$2n$," for example, to be capable of representing any even number and part of the semantic role of the term "A $\vee$ B" to be capable of representing any disjunctive formula. For just as it is characteristic of a closed term such as "2.3" to represent a particular individual, so it is characteristic of an open term, such as "2n," to represent a range of admissible values and, just as the representation of a particular individual is a semantic relationship, so is the representation of a range of admissible values. We would, therefore, appear to have as much reason to regard the representation of a range of individuals as a part of the semantic role of an open term as we have to regard the representation of a particular individual as part of the semantic role of a closed term.

But the opponent of semantic roles for open expressions is unlikely to be impressed with these considerations. For he may argue that, in so far as we think of an open expression as having a semantic role, it is because we think of its variables as being implicitly bound. There is perhaps no need to think of them as being bound by a *quantifier*, but there must at least be some variable-binding operator in the background by means of which the supposed semantic role of the open expression is to be understood. So, for example, the term "2n" might be understood, in so far as it is seen to have a semantic role, as doing duty for the set-term "{2n: n a natural number}" or for the λ-term "λn.2n" (denoting the function from each number to its double).

I do not regard this account of the alleged semantic role of open expressions as at all plausible. The alleged semantic role of open expressions, in terms of its representing a range of values, would appear to be perfectly intelligible quite apart from the possible connection with variable-binding. Indeed, some philosophers have supposed that certain types of variable – or variable-like expression – might not even be subject to quantification or other forms of variable-binding. The schematic letters "A" and "B" of Quine (1952, section 1.5), for example, are meant to "stand in" for the sentences of some language and yet are not bindable on pain of supposing that the sentences are names for some special kind of entity. These schematic letters, as much as regular variables, are subject to the antinomy and yet would appear to have an independent semantic role. Of course, Quine might be mistaken in his reasons for thinking that schematic letters are not bindable, but he is surely not mistaken in thinking that their semantic role can be understood apart from the connection with quantification or other forms of variable binding.

The opponent of semantic roles for open expressions also faces the awkward issue of saying what the implicit binding should be taken to be. One wants to say that a term "$2n$" indifferently represents all even numbers. Our opponent says that the term can only be regarded as having a semantic role in so far as it is implicitly bound. But by what? Two obvious candidates, when no sentential context is at hand, are the set-term "$\{2n: n$ a natural number$\}$" and the λ-term "$\lambda n.2n$"; a less obvious candidate is "the x for which x is even" where this is taken to denote an *arbitrary even number* in the sense of Fine (1985). Thus it must be supposed that an implicit reference and an implicit ontological commitment are made to the set or function or arbitrary object, or to something else of this sort. But this is both arbitrary and gratuitous. For there is no reason to suppose that the implicit reference is to one of these entities as opposed to the other and it appears entirely irrelevant to our use of the term that it should carry any such implicit reference or commitment.

A perhaps even more decisive objection to the position arises from the consideration of semantic relationships. Not only do open expressions appear to have semantic roles, they also appear to enter into semantic relationships. For example, the "value" of the term "$n + 1$" is always greater than the "value" of "n," though not of "m." But how is our opponent to account for these apparent semantic relationships? If he takes the variables of each term, taken on its own, to be implicitly bound, he is sunk: for then "$n + 1$" will signify the successor function, say, and "n" the identity function, and so we will lose the special semantic relationship that holds between "$n + 1$" and "n" as opposed to "$n + 1$" and "m." He must, therefore, take the variables of the two terms to be somehow simultaneously bound. He must say something like: "What accounts for the apparent semantic relationship between '$n + 1$' and 'n' is the fact that the quantified sentence '$\forall n(n + 1 > n)$' is true." But it seems bizarre to suppose that one must create this artificial context in which both terms occur in order to explain the semantic relationship between them. What kind of strange semantic relationship between the terms is it that can only be explained by embedding them within a richer language? Indeed, the proposed explanation of the semantic relationship presupposes that the relevant semantic features of the terms are preserved when they are embedded in the context of a single sentence; and so unless we had some independent way of saying what that semantic relationship was, we would have no way to say what the presupposition was or whether it was correct.

If we are right, then the independent semantic role of open expressions is not to be denied and the antinomy is not to be solved by denying that they have such a role.

D.   The Instantial Approach

I have so far left open the question of whether there might be an autonomous semantics for closed expressions, one not taking a detour through open expressions. I now wish to argue that no such semantics is viable – or, at least, plausible. As I have mentioned, there are two main forms of autonomous semantics, the instantial and the algebraic. The reasons for thinking them unsatisfactory are somewhat different; and so let us consider each in turn.

According to the instantial approach, a closed quantified sentence, such as $\exists x B(x)$ is to be understood on the basis of one of its instances $B(c)$ – the intuitive idea being that from an understanding of $B(c)$, we may acquire an understanding of what it is for an arbitrary individual to satisfy the condition denoted by $B(\ )$ and that, from this, we may then acquire an understanding of what it is for this condition to be satisfied by some individual or other. But although the intuitive idea behind the proposal may be clear, it is far from clear how the proposal is to be made precise.

A certain semantic value is to be assigned to a closed instance $B(c)$ of the existential sentence $\exists x B(x)$. Let us call it a "proposition," though without any commitment as to what it is. A certain "condition" is then to be determined on the basis of this proposition. But how? We took it to be the condition denoted by the scheme $B(\ )$ which results from removing all displayed occurrences of the term c from $B(c)$. This suggests that the condition should likewise be taken to be the result of removing all corresponding occurrences of the individual denoted by c from the given proposition; indeed, we are given no other indication of how the condition might be determined. It must therefore be presupposed that there is an operation of "abstraction" which, in application to any proposition and any occurrences of an individual in that proposition, will result in a certain condition or propositional "form" from which the given occurrences of the individual have been removed. Once given such a form, we may then take the quantified sentence $\exists x B(x)$ to predicate "existence" of it.

Now a great deal more needs to be said about the operation of abstraction before we have a precisely formulated semantics.[5] But one thing is clear. The use of such an operation in formulating the semantics for predicate logic is not compatible with an extensional approach, one in which we take cognizance only of the individuals denoted by the closed terms, the extensions of the predicates, and the truth-values of the sentences. For if there is to be a meaningful operation of abstraction, then the propositions to which it is to be applied must to some extent share in the structure of the sentences by which they are expressed; they must contain individuals in a way analogous to the way in which the sentences contain terms; and it must make sense to remove the individuals from the propositions in a way that is analogous to the removal of terms from a sentence. But, clearly, there is nothing in an extensional approach that would enable us to make sense of such ideas.

So much the worse, one might think, for the extensional approach. But however sympathetic one might be to alternative semantic approaches, it is hard to believe that our current problems lie in the adherence to extensionality. After all, the extensionalist credentials of variables are as good as they get: they simply range over a given domain of individuals without the intervention of different senses for different individuals and without the need for different senses by which the domain might be picked out for different variables. It is, therefore, hard to see why the addition of variables to a language that was otherwise in conformity with extensional principles should give rise to any essentially new difficulties. If the extensional project fails, it cannot be because the variables carry some hidden intensional baggage.[6]

There is, in any case, another, more subtle difficulty with the instantial approach, which not even the intensional form of semantics is able to solve. For it is a mistake to suppose that our understanding of the quantified sentence is *derived* from our understanding of a particular instance, since there may be no particular instance that we are in a position to understand. Suppose, for example, that the variables range over all points in abstract Euclidean space. Then it is impossible to name any particular point. But if we are incapable of understanding any instance of the quantified sentence then, a fortiori, we are incapable of deriving our understanding of the quantified sentence from our understanding of an instance.

Of course, what we really wanted to say was that the understanding of $\exists x B(x)$ should be derived from our understanding of an *arbitrary* instance. We have seen that this should not be taken to mean that our understanding of $\exists x B(x)$ derives from our understanding of some particular instance, though it does not matter which. But then what does it mean?

The only reasonable view seems to be that our understanding of $\exists x B(x)$ should be taken to derive from our general understanding of $B(x)$, i.e. from our understanding of the proposition expressed by $B(x)$ for any given value of the variable x. But the idea of a closed instance then falls by the wayside and we are left with the idea of understanding the quantified sentence $\exists x B(x)$ in terms of the corresponding open sentence $B(x)$. Thus we see that the instantial approach, once properly understood, does not even constitute an autonomous form of semantics.

E.   The Algebraic Approach

Under the alternative autonomous approach, the apparatus of binding is traded in for an algebra of operations, with the apparatus serving, in effect, as a device to indicate how the semantic value for a whole sentence is to be generated from the properties and relations expressed by the primitive predicates that it contains. In this case, there is no difficulty in making the semantics precise or in presenting it in extensional form. But there is a difficulty in seeing how to extend it beyond the standard symbolism of predicate logic.

One difficulty of this sort arises from the use of quantifiers that apply to several variables at once, though in no set order. We might have a quantifier "always," for example, that implicitly binds all variables "in sight." Let us symbolize it by "$\forall$" (without attached variables) and take "$\forall A$" to indicate that "A" holds no matter what values are assumed by the free variables occurring in "A." The question now arises as to how the proponent of the algebraic approach is to understand a (false) sentence such as "$\forall (2x > 3y)$."[7] Clearly, he must understand it in terms of the application of a universality operator to a λ-term constructed from "$2x > 3y$." But which λ-term? There would appear to be only two options: (i) it is a λ-term, such as "$\lambda xy(2x > 3y)$" or "$\lambda yx(2x > 3y)$," in which the variables attached to the λ-symbol are taken to occur in a set order; (ii) it is a λ-term, "$\lambda(2x > 3y)$," in which the λ-symbol is taken, like the quantifier-symbol $\forall$, to apply to all free variables in sight, though in no set order.

But the first option gives a more specific meaning to the sentence than it actually appears to possess, one that involves either the relation $\lambda xy(2x > 3y)$ or the extensionally distinct relation $\lambda yx(2x > 3y)$. We must, therefore, either arbitrarily adopt one interpretation over another or attribute to the sentence an indeterminacy in meaning which it does not have. And one should not think that the relevant order might be given by the standard alphabetic order of the variables or by the order in which they occur in the formula that follows the quantifier, for we might take the variables to be symbols – such as "#" and "*" – which are not alphabetized in any given order and the formula might be written in a nonlinear notation from which no set order of occurrence can be discerned.[8]

The second option is clearly more faithful to our semantic intentions. But it plays havoc with the idea of distributing the binders across the logical connectives. For, on pain of reintroducing an arbitrary order on the variables, a λ-term such as $\lambda(x > y)$ will have to symbolize a relation that is neutral between the "biased" relations symbolized by $\lambda xy(x > y)$ and $\lambda yx(x > y)$.[9] But this means that, when we push the binder λ through $\lambda(x > y \vee y > x)$ in order to obtain the disjunction of the relations symbolized by $\lambda(x > y)$ and $\lambda(y > x)$, we will lose track of the alignment between the variables in the two disjuncts and will, therefore, be unable to distinguish, in the way we should, between $\lambda(x > y \vee y > x)$ and $\lambda(x > y \vee x > y)$.

A similar difficulty arises from the use of modal and other intensional operators. Suppose that we add an operator "$\square$" for necessity to the symbolism for first-order logic and that we take the interpretation of the quantifiers to be "actualist" – ranging, in each possible world, over the objects that exist in that world. Consider now the algebraic treatment of $\lambda x \square(x = x)$ and of $\lambda x \square \exists y(y = x)$. $\lambda x \square(x = x)$ should be understood to signify the result of applying some operation, call it "necessitation," to the property (of self-identity) signified by $\lambda x(x = x)$ and $\lambda x \square \exists y(y = x)$ should be understood to signify the result of applying this same operation to the property (of existence) signified by $\exists y(y = x)$. Under an actualist interpretation of the quantifier (and hence presumably also of λ-binding), $\lambda x(x = x)$ and

$\lambda x \exists y (y = x)$ will be modally indistinguishable – they will be true, in each possible world, of the individuals that exist in that world. And this is plausibly taken to imply, under any natural understanding of $\square$ as a modal operator, that $\lambda x \square (x = x)$ and of $\lambda x \exists y (y = x)$ should also be modally indistinguishable. But they *are* modally distinguishable, since the first is true of any individual whatever (given that identity is not existence-entailing) while the second is only true of individuals that necessarily exist. The general point is that the success of the algebraic approach depends upon presupposing the truth of certain "distribution" principles and there is no reason, in general, to suppose that such principles will be true. Of course, one might still apply the algebraic approach to those languages for which the relevant distribution principles hold. But this would be a kind of lucky accident, since a satisfactory account of quantification should be of general import and not depend for its success upon special features of the language to which it is applied.

Another serious difficulty with the approach is that it requires us, at almost every turn, to make arbitrary decisions about the interpretation of the symbolism which have no counterpart in our actual understanding of the symbolism. Let me merely give one illustration. When we push the λ-operators through logically complex formulas, we will eventually reach λ-terms of the form $\lambda x_1 x_2 \ldots x_m F y_1 y_2 \ldots y_n$, in which the binder $\lambda x_1 x_2 \ldots x_m$ governs an atomic formula $F y_1 y_2 \ldots y_n$ (where some of the variables $x_1, x_2, \ldots, x_m$ may, of course, be the same as one another and the same as some of the variables $y_1, y_2, \ldots, y_n$). How then are these terms to be interpreted?

Presumably, in keeping with the algebraic approach, we should take $\lambda x_1 x_2 \ldots x_m F y_1 y_2 \ldots y_n$ to signify the result of applying some operation to the relation F signified by the predicate F. So, for example, $\lambda x F x x$ will signify the reflexive version of F, while $\lambda y x F x y$ will signify the converse of F (at least, if $\lambda x y F x y$ signifies F itself). But what of the operation itself? It must presumably be determined on the basis of the relative disposition of the variables $x_1 x_2 \ldots x_m$ in the binder and of the variables $y_1 y_2 \ldots y_n$ in the atomic formula. But there are different ways in which this might be done; and nothing to choose between them. Consider $\lambda z x F x x z$, for example. We could take this to be the result of first forming the generalized converse $\lambda z x y F x y z$ of $\lambda x y z F x y z$ and then forming the reflexive version $\lambda z x F x x z$ of the converse, or we could take it to be the result of first forming the reflexive version $\lambda xzFxxz$ of $\lambda xyzFxyz$ and then forming the converse $\lambda zxFxxz$ of the reflexive version; and similarly, and to a much greater degree, for other cases. These choices do not correspond to anything in our actual understanding of the symbolism; and so, again, we face the awkward choice of making the interpretation either arbitrarily specific or unacceptably indeterminate.

The algebraic approach is best viewed as an attempt to see the symbolism of first-order logic as something which it is not. What it provides, in effect, is a translation from a language with variables to one without variables. A λ-term such as $\lambda zxFxxz$, for example, may be taken to be equivalent in meaning to the term Refl(Conv(F)), indicating the application of reflexive and converse operations to the relation signified by F; and all appeal to variables in the target language is thereby made to disappear. But in making the transition to a variable-free notation, not only are we forced to make arbitrary decisions about how the translation should go, we thereby loose what is most distinctive about the use of variables. For instead of being treated as devices of reference, albeit of a special sort, they are treated as more or less oblique ways to indicate the application of various operations within a calculus of relations. The problem of understanding our use of variables is not solved but side-stepped.

F. The Relational Approach

I now wish to indicate how I think the antinomy is to be solved and how a more satisfactory semantics for the symbolism of first-order logic might thereby be developed.

I agree with the autonomous approach in thinking that the formulation of the antinomy embodies a false presupposition. But the false presupposition lies not in the attribution of a semantic role to free variables but in the presumption that there is conflict between the sameness in semantic role of x and y, on the one hand, and the difference in semantic role of x, y and x, x, on the other (SS' and SD' above).

There are, I believe, two things that stand in the way of our seeing how these attributions of sameness and difference might be reconciled. The first concerns a possible ambiguity in the notion of semantic role. We have already had occasion to distinguish between sameness or difference of semantic role *across* contexts and *within* a given context. But there is, I believe, another ambiguity in the notion of semantic role that might stand in the way of seeing how reconciliation is to be achieved.

This may be brought to light by considering the following argument against the possibility of reconciliation. Suppose, in conformity with SD′, that the semantic roles of the pair x, y and of the pair x, x are not the same. Then it may be argued that the semantic roles of the individual variables x and y cannot be the same, in contradiction to SS′. For x, when paired with x, has the same semantic role as x, x whereas y, when paired with x, does not have the same semantic role as x, x. The variables, therefore, differ in respect of whether their pairing with x gives something with the same semantic role as x, x.

It is not to be denied that there is a semantic difference of the presumed sort between x and y. But it is not in this sense that we wish to deny that there is a semantic difference between x and y. To see how this is so, let us distinguish between the *intrinsic* (or non-relational) and the *extrinsic* (or relational) semantic features of an expression. The intrinsic semantic features of an expression, in contrast to its extrinsic semantic features, do not concern its semantic relationship to other expressions. Thus it will be an intrinsic semantic feature of the predicate "doctor" that it is true of doctors but not an intrinsic semantic feature that it is synonymous with "physician." Likewise, the intrinsic semantic features of a *pair* of expressions will consist of those semantic relationships between the expressions which do not concern their semantic relationship to yet further expressions. Thus it will be an intrinsic semantic feature of the pair "doctor" and "physician" that they are synonymous, though not that they are both synonymous with "licensed medical practitioner."

Now what the above argument shows is that if there is an intrinsic semantic difference between the pairs of variables x, y and x, x, then there will be an extrinsic semantic difference between the individual variables x and y themselves (concerning the relationship of each to the variable x). But in asserting that the semantic role of x and y is the same, we only wish to assert that their intrinsic semantic features are the same; and in asserting that the semantic roles of x, y and x, x are different, we only wish to assert that their intrinsic semantic features are different. Thus the present difficulty will not arise as long as we always take semantic role to be intrinsic.

The other impediment to achieving reconciliation rests upon a mistake in doctrine rather than upon a failure to recognize a distinction. Let it be granted that the relevant notion of semantic role is both cross-contextual and intrinsic. Still, it might be thought, how can there be a difference in the (intrinsic) semantic relationships holding between each of two pairs of expressions without there being a difference in the intrinsic semantic features of the expressions themselves? Thus given a difference in semantic relationship between the pairs "doctor", "dentist" and "doctor", "doctor" (with the one being pair synonymous and the other not), there must be a difference in meaning between "doctor" and "dentist." Similarly, given that there is a difference in semantic relationship between the pairs of variables x, y and x, x, must there not be a difference in "meaning" between x and y?

According to this point of view, there can be no difference in intrinsic semantic relationship without a difference in intrinsic semantic feature. All differences in meaning must be attributable to intrinsic differences; and any attempt to reconcile the attributions of semantic sameness and difference is doomed to failure.

It has to be acknowledged that this view of meaning – what we might call "semantical intrinsicalism" – seems hard to dispute. But it is false all the same; and a careful examination of the behavior of variables indicates how. For suppose again, to fix our ideas, that we are dealing with a language that contains the variables x_1, x_2, x_3, . . . How then is their semantic behavior to be described?

We should certainly specify the range of values each variable can assume and, given that the language is "one-sorted," the range of values for each variable will then be the same. Now it might be thought that the specification of the range is sufficient to fix the behavior of the variables. But this is not strictly so. For we should specify not only which values each *single* variable can assume, when taken on its own, but also which values *several* variables can assume, when taken together. We should specify, for example, not only that x_1 can assume the number 2 as a value, say, and x_2 the number 3 but also that x_1 and x_2 can *simultaneously* assume the numbers 2 and 3 as values; and, in general, we should state that the variables take their values independently of one another, that a variable can take any value from its range regardless of which values the other variables might assume.

What is important to appreciate here is that it does not follow, simply from the specification of a range of values for each variable, which values the variables can *simultaneously* assume. One might adopt the proposal of Wittgenstein (1922), for example, and disallow distinct variables from taking the same value; or, at the other extreme, one might insist that distinct variables should always assume the same value (treating them, in effect, as strict notational variants of one another); and there are, of course, numerous other possibilities. Thus the fact that distinct variables assume values in complete independence of one another is an additional piece of information concerning their semantic behavior, one not already implicit in the specification of their range.

However, once we have specified the range of the variables and the independence in their value, we will then have a complete description of their semantic behavior; there is nothing more (at least at the extensional level) to be said about their role. But if this is so, then it is clear that the intrinsicalist doctrine, *no difference in semantic relationship without a difference in semantic feature*, will fail. For the intrinsic semantic features of any two variables will be the same – it will in effect be given by the specification of their range, whereas the intrinsic semantic features of the pairs x_1, x_2, say, and x_1, x_1 will be different, since the former will assume *any* pair of values from the given range while the latter will only assume *identical* pairs of values. If we are merely informed of the intrinsic semantic features of two variables, we cannot, therefore, tell whether they assume their values independently of one another (should they be distinct) or whether they always assume the same value (should they be same).

It is thus by giving up the intrinsicalist doctrine, plausible as it initially appears to be, that the antinomy is to be solved. We must allow that any two variables will be semantically the same, even though pairs of identical and of distinct variables are semantically different; and we should, in general, be open to the possibility that the meaning of the expressions of a language is to be given in terms of their semantic relationships to one another.

Formally, the situation is analogous to failures in the identity of indiscernibles. Consider, for example, the distinct but indiscernible spheres of Max Black (1970). Just as there is no intrinsic spatial difference between the two spheres (once we reject absolute space), so there is no intrinsic semantic difference between two variables. And just as there may be an intrinsic spatial difference between two pairs of spheres – since identical spheres will be coincident whereas distinct spheres will not be, so there may be an intrinsic semantical difference between pairs of variables. From this perspective, then, the lesson to be drawn from the antinomy is that semantics provides another, though less familiar, example of an aspect of "reality" in which things can only be distinguished in terms of their relations to one another, and not solely in terms of their intrinsic features.

G.   Relational Semantics for First-order Logic

Given a relational view of variables, how should the semantics for the language of first-order logic proceed? Let us begin with some general remarks on the proper form of semantics and then consider their application to the case at hand.

The aim of the semantics, as standardly conceived, is to assign a semantic value to each (meaningful) expression of the language under consideration. Suppose that an expression E is syntactically derived from the simpler expressions $E_1, E_2, \ldots, E_m$. Then the semantic value $|E|$ of E is taken to be the appropriate function $f(|E_1|, |E_2|, \ldots, |E_m|)$ of the semantic values of the simpler expressions. Given semantic values for the lexical items of the language (those not derived from other expressions), the semantic value of each expression is then determined.

The aim of a relational semantics, by contrast, is to assign a semantic connection to each sequence of expressions. Such a connection is intended to encapsulate not only the semantic features of each individual expression but also the semantic relationships between them. The semantic value $|E|$ of an expression E is then taken to be a function $f(|E_1, E_2, \ldots, E_m|)$ of the semantic connection $|E_1, E_2, \ldots, E_m|$ on the expressions $E_1, E_2, \ldots, E_m$ from which it is derived and, in general, the semantic connection $|F_1, F_2, \ldots, E, \ldots, F_{n-1}, F_n|$ on the sequence $F_1, F_2, \ldots, E, \ldots, F_{n-1}, F_n$ is taken to be a function $f(|F_1, F_2, \ldots, E_1, E_2, \ldots, E_m, \ldots, F_{n-1}, F_n|)$ of the semantic connection on the simpler sequence $F_1, F_2, \ldots, E_1, E_2, \ldots, E_m, \ldots, F_{n-1}, F_n$, in which E gives way to $E_1, E_2, \ldots, E_m$. Given semantic connections on sequences of lexical items, the semantic connection on any sequence of expressions is then determined. Thus semantic connections replace semantic values as the principal objects of semantic enquiry.

Compositionality, as it is usually formulated, must now be given up. For the "meaning" (or semantic value) of an expression E will not in general be a function of the meanings of its component expressions E_1, E_2, ... , E_m; for the meaning relationships between E_1, E_2, ... , E_m will also be relevant to the meaning of E. But compositionality, more generally conceived, will still hold. The meaning of an expression E will still be a function of the meaning of the component expressions E_1, E_2, ... , E_m, as long as this is construed collectively so as to include the meaning relationships among the different components and not just their individual meanings; and compositionality, so understood, will still enable us to trace the meanings of expressions back to the lexicon, as long as the lexicon is also taken to have a relational semantics. From the present point of view, our previous formulation of compositionality should be seen to be the product of this more general formulation and the intrinsicalist doctrine that the collective meaning of the component expressions is exhausted by their individual meanings. Thus it is only intrinsicalism that is given up, not compositionality proper.

Let us now apply the general idea of a relational semantics to the language of first-order logic. Our first task is to specify the syntax upon which the semantics is to be based. For the most part, this is standard: a disjunctive formula (A ∨ B), for example, will be syntactically derived from the disjunction operator "∨" and the disjuncts A and B, and an atomic sentence $Pt_1t_2 \ldots t_n$ from the predicate P and the argument-terms t_1, t_2, ... , t_n. However, in two key respects the syntax is not altogether standard. In the first place, the lexicon will now be taken to include variables, to which semantic values or connections should be assigned. In the second place, a quantified expression, such as $\exists x A$, will be taken to derive from the quantifier $\exists$, the bound variable x, and the embedded formula A. Thus the bound variable x comes into its own as one of the syntactic constituents of the formula. Such an analysis might appear somewhat naive from a modern perspective, but I actually consider it a strong point in favor of the present approach.

In order to set up the semantics, we need an appropriate conception of semantic connection. This may be obtained, I believe, by generalizing the notion of a value range for a variable. The value range of a variable is the set of values it is capable of assuming. Similarly, given a sequence of expressions, we may take its value range – or semantic connection – to be the set of sequences of values that the expressions are simultaneously capable of assuming. So, for example, the semantic connection on "$x + y$," "$x > y$," "z" will include the sequences 5, FALSE, 6 (obtained under the assignment of 2 to "x," 3 to "y," and 6 to "z") and the sequence 6, TRUE, 2 (obtained under the assignment of 4 to "x," 2 to "y," and 2 to "z"). It should be noted that the semantic connections are entirely non-typographic; they contain no trace of the expressions from which they were derived and there is, therefore, no danger of the semantics being implicitly typographic.

We must now show how to determine the semantic connection on any given sequence of expressions – starting with the lexical semantics, for the very simplest expressions, and then successively working our way through more and more complicated forms of expression. The lexical semantics is, for the most part, straightforward: extensions should be assigned to predicates, denotations to constants, and functions to function symbols. However, we now include variables within the lexicon and so the lexical semantics should also specify the semantic connection on any sequence of variables. Suppose that we are given the sequence of variables x, y, x, y, for example. Then in conformity with our understanding that distinct variables take values independently of one another and that identical variables take the same value, the semantic connection on this sequence should be the set of all quadruples a, b, c, d of individuals from the domain for which $a = c$ and $b = d$. And, in general, the semantic connection on the variables $x_1, x_2 \ldots, x_n$ should be taken to be the set of all n-tples $a_1, a_2 \ldots, a_n$ of individuals from the domain for which $a_i = a_j$ whenever $x_i = x_j$ ($1 \leq i < j \leq n$). It is at this point that relationism first enters the semantic scene.

We also need rules for extending the semantic connections to more complicated expressions and more complicated sequences of expressions. Consider, by way of example, the complex terms $x.x$ and $x.y$. The first should have as its value-range the set of all non-negative reals (given that the variables range over reals); and the second should have as its value-range the set of all reals whatever. But how do we secure this result? If we let the value-range of $x.x$ simply be a function of the value-range of x and x, and similarly for $x.y$, then we cannot distinguish between them, since the value-ranges of x and y are the same. However, we have taken the value-range of $x.x$ to be a function of the semantic connection on x, x and the value-range of $x.y$ to be a function of the semantic connection on x, y. These semantic connections differ, as we have seen, the first comprising all identical pairs of reals and the second comprising all pairs of reals whatever. There is, therefore, a corresponding difference in the value ranges of $x.x$ and $x.y$; for each will comprise the corresponding set of products and will thereby yield the required difference in result.

More generally, let us suppose that we have a complex term $ft_1t_2 \ldots t_n$ and that we wish to determine the semantic connection on a sequence of expressions involving the term. The general form of such a sequence will be $D_1, D_2 \ldots D_p, ft_1t_2 \ldots t_n, E_1, E_2, \ldots, E_q$ (with $p, q \geq 0$). Now, under the standard approach to semantics, the semantic value of the complex term $ft_1t_2 \ldots t_n$ will be determined on the basis of the semantic value f of its function symbol f and the semantic values $a_1, a_2, \ldots a_n$ (under a given assignment) of its argument-terms $t_1, t_2, \ldots, t_n$; and this semantic value will be taken to be the result $f(a_1, a_2, \ldots a_n)$ of applying the function f to the arguments a_1, $a_2, \ldots a_n$. This suggests that the semantic connection on the sequence $D_1, D_2 \ldots D_p, ft_1t_2 \ldots t_n, E_1, E_2, \ldots, E_q$ should be determined on the basis of the semantic connection on $D_1, D_2 \ldots D_p, f, t_1, t_2, \ldots t_n, E_1$, $E_2, \ldots, E_q$ (with $ft_1t_2 \ldots t_n$ giving way, as before, to f, $t_1, t_2, \ldots, t_n$); and $d_1, d_2, \ldots d_p, b, e_1, e_2, \ldots, e_q$ will belong to the semantic connection on $D_1, D_2 \ldots D_p, ft_1t_2 \ldots t_n, E_1, E_2, \ldots E_q$, i.e. $ft_1t_2 \ldots t_n$ will be capable of taking the value b when $D_1, D_2 \ldots D_p, E_1, E_2, \ldots$, E_q take the values $d_1, d_2, \ldots d_p, e_1, e_2, \ldots, e_q$, just in case, for some individuals $a_1, a_2, \ldots, a_n$ for which $b = f(a_1, a_2, \ldots a_n)$, $t_1, t_2, \ldots t_n$ are capable of taking the values $a_1, a_2, \ldots a_n$ when $D_1, D_2 \ldots D_p, E_1, E_2, \ldots, E_q$ take the values $d_1, d_2, \ldots d_p, e_1$, $e_2, \ldots, e_q$, i.e. just in case, for some individuals $a_1, a_2, \ldots a_n$ for which $b = f(a_1, a_2, \ldots a_n)$, the tple $d_1, d_2, \ldots d_p, f, a_1, a_2, \ldots, a_n, e_1, e_2, \ldots$, e_q belongs to the semantic connection on $D_1, D_2 \ldots D_p, f, t_1, t_2, \ldots t_n$, $E_1, E_2, \ldots, E_q$.

The above rule is easily extended to the case of atomic formulas; and a similar rule may be given in the case of truth-functionally complex formulas. The semantic connection on $\sim A$, E, for example, will consist of all those pairs π', e for which π, e is a member of the semantic connection on A, E and π' is the "complementary" truth-value to π.

Quantifiers raise additional problems. The obvious way of evaluating a sequence containing a quantified formula – such as $\exists x A(x)$, E – is in terms of the connection on x, $A(x)$, E. If, for a fixed semantic value of E, $A(x)$ is true for the assignment of some individual from the domain to "x," then $\exists x A(x)$ should be taken to be true and otherwise should be taken to be false. Thus the pair TRUE, e will belong to the connection on $\exists x A(x)$, E just in case, for some individual a from the domain, the triple a, TRUE, e belongs to the connection on x, $A(x)$, E (and similarly for the pair FALSE, e).[10]

But consider how such a rule applies to a sequence of the form $\exists x A(x)$, x – say to $\exists x(x > 0)$, x (where the domain of quantification is the set of all natural numbers). The pair TRUE, 0 will belong to the semantic connection on $\exists x(x > 0)$, x just in case, for some natural number n, the triple n, TRUE, 0 belongs to the semantic connection on x, $x > 0$, x. But since the first and third variables in x, $x > 0$, x are the same, the first and third components of any triple in its semantic connection will be the same. It follows that no triple of the form n, TRUE, 0 can belong to the semantic connection on x, $x > 0$, x and so the pair TRUE, 0 will not belong to the semantic connection on $\exists x(x > 0)$, x – contrary to our intentions.

The problem is that we do not want the bound occurrences of the variable x in $\exists x A(x)$, x to be "coordinated" with the free occurrence. However, our method of evaluation requires that they be coordinated since $\exists x A(x)$, x is evaluated in terms of x, $A(x)$, x. What makes the problem especially acute is that we wish to subject $\exists x(x > 0)$, x to essentially the same method of evaluation as $\exists y(y > 0)$, x, since they are mere notational variants of one another, and yet we also want to subject $\exists y(y > 0)$, x to the straightforward evaluation in terms of y, $y > 0$, x.

The way out of the impasse, I believe, is to give up the assumption that all occurrences of the same variable should be treated in the same way. We have so far assumed that different free occurrences of the same variable should always take the same individual as value; and this is, indeed, a reasonable default assumption to make. However, when a free occurrence of a variable was previously bound and only became free in the process of evaluation, then we should no longer assume that it is coordinated with those occurrences of the same variable that were either originally free or had their origin in a different quantifier.

This means that, for the purpose of evaluating a sequence of expressions, we should explicitly indicate which of the free occurrences of a given variable are to be coordinated and which not. In the sequence x, $x > 0$, x, for example, we should distinguish between the cases in which none of the occurrences of x are to be coordinated, in which all are, or in which only two are. The reader might picture these coordinating links as lines connecting one occurrence of the variable to another, just as in the "telegraphic" notation for predicate logic.[11]

This then provides us with the means of evaluating $\exists x(x > 0)$, x in terms of x, $x > 0$, x, in strict analogy with the evaluation of $\exists y(y > 0)$, x in terms of y, $y > 0$, x. However, in order for this to be possible, the variables in the evaluating sequences should be subject to the appropriate pattern of coordination; the first two occurrences of x in x, $x > 0$, x should be coordinated with one another (though not with the third occurrence) and the first two occurrences of y in y, $y > 0$, x should likewise be coordinated. In general, whenever we are evaluating a quantified formula $\exists x A(x)$ in terms of its components x, $A(x)$ within the context of a sequence, the designated occurrences of x should be taken to be coordinated with one another, though not with any other occurrences of x that may happen to be present in the sequence.

Modest as this proposal might appear to be, its development calls for some fundamental revisions in the previous formulation of the syntax and the semantics. In the first place, the syntactic object of evaluation will no longer be a sequence of expressions but a *coordinated* sequence of expressions. This is a sequence of expressions E_1, E_2, ... E_n along with a *coordination scheme* $\mathcal{C}$ which tells us when two free occurrences of the same variable are to be coordinated (formally, a coordination scheme is an equivalence relation on the free occurrences of variables in the sequence subject to the requirement that it only relate occurrences of the same variable.) The syntactic rules must then be appropriately modified. The formula $\exists x A$, for example, should be taken to derive, not simply from $\exists$, x and A but from a sequence of expressions $\exists$, x and A in which the first occurrence of the variable x is coordinated with all of the free occurrences of x in A; the binding lives on, as it were, in the syntactic derivation of the formula. In the second place, the lexical rule for the variables must be modified. Instead of requiring that all occurrences of the same variable should receive the same value, we should only require that they receive the same value when they are coordinated. Thus the syntax itself becomes relational and coordination at the semantic level should be seen to reflect an underlying coordination at the level of the syntax.

I believe that considerable interest attaches to developing the syntax, semantics and proof theory of predicate logic along relational lines, making explicit use of coordination at the level both of syntax and of semantics.[12] Let me here just mention one possible line of investigation (another will be discussed in connection with the use of quantified epistemic logic in section G of chapter 4). Students of logic often have difficulty in interpreting the formula $(\exists x Px \wedge Qx)$. They take it to have the same truth-conditions as $\exists x(Px \wedge Qx)$ rather than treating the third occurrence of x as a dangling variable. Their mistake is understandable if ordinary language is their guide, since "I met a man and he was wearing a bowler hat" is naturally taken to have the same truth-conditions as "I met a man who was wearing a bowler hat." The so-called "dynamic" semantics for predicate logic accounts for the student's interpretation of $(\exists x Px \wedge Qx)$ but does not sit well with the standard "static" interpretation. The question, therefore, arises as to whether there is a general framework that might accommodate both interpretations, with each the result of some "tweaking" in the value of some "parameter." Relationism provides such a framework. For the semantic value of $(\exists x Px \wedge Qx)$ will depend upon the semantic connection on $\exists x Px$, $\wedge$, Qx, which, in its turn, will depend upon the semantic connection on $\exists$, x, Px, $\wedge$, Qx. But we now face the question as to whether, in dismantling the quantifier expression, the first two occurrences of x should or should not be coordinated with the third occurrence. If they are, we obtain the nonstandard dynamic interpretation; and if they are not, we obtain the standard static interpretation. The relational framework can be used in other ways to provide alternative interpretations of the quantifiers; and it is perhaps a great virtue of the approach that it is able to account in a systematic way for these differences in interpretation.

We see, in conclusion, that the relational semantics for the language of first-order logic has several clear advantages over its rivals. First and foremost, it embodies a solution to the antinomy:

the intrinsic semantic features of x and y (as given by the degenerate semantic connections on those variables) are the same, though the intrinsic semantic features of the pairs x, y and x, x (again, as given by the semantic connections on those pairs) are different. The semantics is also more satisfactory, in various ways, *as* a semantics. In contrast to the autonomous approaches, it assigns a semantic role to open expressions; in contrast to the instantial approach, it can be given an extensional formulation; and in contrast to the algebraic approach, it is based upon a credible direct method of evaluation. It also has the great advantage – over its main rival, the Tarski semantics – of not being typographic. By going relational, we avoid having to incorporate the variables themselves (or some surrogate thereof) into the very identity of the entities that the semantics assigns to the open expressions of the language.

Chapter 2

Coordination within Language

An examination of the semantics of first-order logic has revealed the existence of irreducible semantic relationships among variables, i.e. of semantic relationships not grounded in the intrinsic semantic features of the variables themselves. This suggests that the existence of such relationships may not be peculiar to this case and that there may be other kinds of expression or representational device to which some sort of relationism will apply. The remaining chapters are largely devoted to an exploration of this question – beginning with names and then moving to the constituents of thought and the semantics of belief reports.

Just as the focus of the previous chapter was on the antinomy of the variable, the focus of the present chapter is on Frege's broadly analogous puzzle concerning names (section A). This puzzle has been much discussed but I shall argue that none of the existing responses is satisfactory and that it is only by going relational that the semantical version of the puzzle can be solved (section B). Critical to the line of argument is a certain conception of semantics. For it is only by thinking of semantics as a body of information rather than of fact that the relevant distinctions can be made out and a viable form of relationism defended (sections C and D). After reviewing the relational solution to the puzzle (section E), I present a relational semantics for names in analogy to the relational semantics for variables (section F) and argue that, in contrast to standard referentialism, the relational referentialist is able to respect the "transparency" of meaning (section G).

A.   Frege's Puzzle

We begin with a statement of Frege's famous puzzle concerning identity sentences (I make no claim to historical accuracy). First, some terminology by means of which the puzzle may be stated. Say that two sentences are *cognitively different* if they can convey different information to someone who understands both sentences; say that two meaningful expressions are *semantically different* if they differ in their meaning or "semantic role"; and say that two referring expressions are *referentially different* if they are not coreferential.

Take two coreferential names – say, the names "Cicero" and "Tully" for the famous Roman orator; and consider the identity-sentences, "Cicero = Cicero" and "Cicero = Tully." The puzzle may then be seen to be based upon the following five assumptions:

1a   *Cognitive Difference*: The two identity sentences are cognitively different;

1b   *Cognitive Link*: If the sentences are cognitively different, then they are semantically different;

2   *Compositionality*: If the sentences are semantically different, then the names "Cicero" and "Tully" are semantically different;

3   *Referential Link*: If the names "Cicero" and "Tully" are semantically different, they are referentially different;

4   *Referential Identity*: The names "Cicero" and "Tully" are not referentially different.

The five assumptions are jointly inconsistent; and so at least one of them should be given up. The challenge presented by the puzzle is to say which and why.

There is an abridged version of the puzzle, in which Cognitive Difference and Cognitive Link are replaced by the following consequence of them:

1   *Semantic Difference*: The two identity sentences are semantically different.

I shall here be concerned with the abridged, purely semantical, version of the puzzle. It is only later (chapter 3, section D), that I shall take up the cognitive version of the puzzle.

There have been two main responses to the puzzle – the Fregean and the Referentialist. Both sides accept Compositionality and Referential Identity. The only remaining alternatives are therefore to reject Semantic Difference (there is a semantic difference in the identity sentences) or Referential Link (no semantic difference without a referential difference). The Fregeans reject Referential Link but accept Semantic Difference: they maintain that, even though the reference of the names "Cicero" and "Tully" is the same, their meaning or "sense" is different; and given that *their* meaning is different then so, plausibly, is the meaning of the identity-sentences. The Referentialists, on the other hand, reject Semantic Difference but accept Referential Link: for them, there is no more to the meaning or semantic role of a name than its referent; and given that the meaning of the names is the same then so, plausibly, is the meaning of the identity sentences.

Let me provide an (all too) brief review of some of the considerations for and against these two responses. The endorsement of Semantic Difference is a strong point in favor of the Fregean response. We have an intuitive notion of meaning and it seems evident, for this intuitive notion, that the two identity-sentences differ in their meaning. Indeed, the difference is not even of a slight or subtle sort; and it is a major mark against the referentialist view that it does not respect these strong and striking intuitions.[1]

There is also a strong *argument* in favor of Semantic Difference. For even if the intuitive evidence in its favor is rejected, it barely seems possible to reject the intuitive evidence in favor of Cognitive Difference; for surely one may learn something different upon being told "Cicero = Tully" and upon being told "Cicero = Cicero." But it is hard to see how to account for this possible cognitive difference except in terms of a semantic difference.

The main problem with the Fregean position, to my mind, is to say, in particular cases, what the difference in the meaning or sense of the names might plausibly be taken to be. Although there appear to be good theoretical reasons for thinking that there *must* be a difference, it seems hard to say in particular cases what it is. For as Kripke (1980) has pointed out, it seems possible for a speaker, or for speakers, to associate the same beliefs or information with two names, such as "Cicero" and "Tully." And if the information or beliefs are the same, then how can the sense be different?

The Fregeans have been very resourceful in coming up with possible differences in sense for the problem cases that have been raised against them. They have appealed, for example, to the sense that others might attach to the name or to something meta-linguistic, like *the referent of this name*. And so it may be worth mentioning a case that would appear to be resistant to counter-moves of this sort. The inspiration for the case is our previous example of a mini-semantic-universe in which there are two variables that are intrinsically the same and yet relationally different. Given the existence of such an example for variables, one naturally wonders whether there might not exist a similar kind of example for names.

To this end, let us imagine a universe that is completely symmetric around someone's center of vision. Whatever she sees to her left *is* and *looks* qualitatively identical to something she sees on her right (not that she conceptualizes the two sides as "left" and "right" since that would introduce an asymmetry). She is now introduced to two identical twins, one to her left and the other to her right, and she simultaneously names each of them "Bruce"; using a left token of "Bruce" for the left twin and a right token of "Bruce" for the right twin. The two tokens of "Bruce" are then always used in tandem so as not to disturb the symmetry. Thus if she uses a left token of "Bruce" to say "Bruce is wearing pink pajamas," she simultaneously uses a right token of "Bruce" to utter the same thing. She can even assert the non-identity of the two Bruces by simultaneously uttering the one token of "Bruce" from the left side of her mouth, the other token from the right, and a word for non-identity from the middle of her mouth.

It seems intuitively clear that she has the use of two names or, at least, the ambiguous use of a single name; and this is something that the Fregean should in any case accept since the name or names can be used to state an informative identity.[2] But what, then, is the difference in sense? By considerations of symmetry, there is no purely descriptive difference in the referents. And this in itself is enough to refute a view that takes sense to be a purely descriptive means of identifying a referent. We can even suppose that she is originally introduced to one person but, seeing him "double," takes him to be two people. Her use of the two names will then not even differ in their reference.

But what of a more liberal view of sense, one that allows it to be partly nondescriptive?[3] Given that our subject "picks out" the object or objects in two different ways, then might this not be taken to constitute a difference in sense? But what exactly are these different ways of picking out the objects meant to be? There would appear to be only two plausible candidates. They could be ways in which the objects are *currently* picked out; the sense of a token of a name, in other words, would somehow be tied to the use of that very token (or perhaps to the preceding token). But in this case, the sense of the name would vary from one moment to the next; and yet surely this is not so – or, at the very least, surely it should be possible for our subject to use consecutive tokens of the name in the very same way and hence with the very same sense. The other alternative is to look at the ways in which the two names were *originally* picked out; the sense of each token of the names would then be tied to the original identification of the objects. The problem here is that it would appear to be compatible with the continued use of each name that the subject should irretrievably lose all knowledge of how its referent was originally identified; and, in this case, she would be put in the bizarre situation of being able to use the name without having any knowledge, or even possible knowledge, of how it was to be understood. But neither option is plausible in itself; and nor would it be congenial to the Fregean, who would want to insist upon our ability to reproduce and access the sense of the words we use.

B.   Rejecting Compositionality

Current philosophical thinking on Frege's puzzles has reached an impasse, with strong theoretical arguments in favor of Semantic Difference and strong intuitive arguments in favor of Referential Link and yet no apparent way to choose between them. And this suggests that we should perhaps take more seriously the possibility of rejecting the assumption of Compositionality that puts them in conflict. For we might then affirm both that there is no semantic difference between coreferential names, thereby securing the benefits of the referentialist position, and that there is a semantic (or cognitive) difference between the identity-sentences, thereby securing the benefits of the Fregean position. A more acceptable form of referentialism might thereby be embraced, not subject to the usual Fregean objections.

But how is Compositionality plausibly to be rejected? It is at this point, I believe, that our previous considerations concerning the semantical role of variables may prove helpful. For consider the analogue for variables of Frege's puzzle for names:

1′   The identity-formulas "$x = x$" and "$x = y$" are semantically different (have a different semantical role);

2′   If the identity-formulas are semantically different, then so are the variables "x" and "y";

3′   The variables "x" and "y" are not semantically different.

As before, the assumptions are jointly inconsistent; and so one of them must be given up.

However, in the present case, neither the Fregean nor the referentialist response is at all plausible. We can hardly toe the referentialist line by denying 1′, for clearly there is a difference in semantical role between the formulas "$x = x$" and "$x = y$." But nor can we toe the Fregean line by denying 3′, for in what could the semantic difference between the variables "x" and "y" consist? It is not as if the variables "x" and "y" have a special "x"-sense or "y"-sense not possessed by the other. Thus it looks in this case as if the only reasonable option is to reject Compositionality.

The relational approach to variables also helps to make plausible *how* Compositionality might be rejected. For, as I have noted, we should distinguish between "Compositionality Proper" and "Intrinsicality." Compositionality Proper, in the present case, requires:

2′(a)   If the identity formulas "$x = x$" and "$x = y$" are semantically different, then so are the pairs of variables x, x and x, y.

Intrinsicality, on the other hand, requires:

2′(b)   If the pairs x, x and x, y are semantically different, then so are the variables x and y.

But we may give up Intrinsicality without giving up Compositionality Proper; and as long as we have Compositionality Proper, we are still able to provide a relational semantics for the use of variables. Thus rejection of Compositionality, as originally stated, does not require that we reject the general idea of a compositional semantics; and so the principal reason for adhering to Compositionality is removed.

This suggests that we might be able to say something similar in the case of names. Compositionality Proper now takes the form:

2(a)   If the identity-sentences "Cicero = Cicero" and "Cicero = Tully" are semantically different, then so are the pairs of names "Cicero", "Cicero" and "Cicero", "Tully";

while Intrinsicality takes the form:

2(b)   If the pairs of names "Cicero", "Cicero" and "Cicero", "Tully" are semantically different then so are the names "Cicero" and "Tully."

And so it looks as if we might reject Compositionality by rejecting Intrinsicality without thereby giving up the idea of a compositional semantics for the use of names.

Unfortunately, the analogy with variables will only take us so far. For it requires that, even though there be no semantic difference between the names "Cicero" and "Tully," there should be a semantic difference between the pairs of names "Cicero", "Cicero" and "Cicero", "Tully." There should, in other words, be a semantic relationship that holds between "Cicero" and "Cicero" yet not between "Cicero" and "Tully." But what might that relationship be? In the case of variables, we could appeal to the evident fact that the variables "x" and "x" take "coordinated" values whereas the variables "x" and "y" take their values independently of one another. But in the case of names, the semantic role of each coreferential name is already fixed by its referent and so talk of "coordination" or "independence" would appear to be out of place.

If one attempts to say what this relationship between the names might be, then one is tempted to say something along the following lines. The names "Cicero" and "Cicero" in the identity-sentence "Cicero = Cicero" both represent the same object, as do the names "Cicero" and "Tully" in the identity "Cicero = Tully." But the first pair of names represents the object *as the same* whereas the second pair does not. In the first case, as opposed to the second, it is somehow part of how the names represent their objects that the objects should be the same.

I take it that we all have some intuitive grip on this notion of coordination or *representing as the same*. But a good test of when an object is represented as the same is in terms of whether one might sensibly raise the question of whether it *is* the same. An object is represented as the same in a piece of discourse only if no one who understands the discourse can sensibly raise the question of whether it is the same. Suppose that you say "Cicero is an orator" and later say "Cicero was honest," intending to make the very same use of the name "Cicero." Then anyone who raises the question of whether the reference was the same would thereby betray his lack of understanding of what you meant.

The idea of representing objects *as* the same is to be distinguished from the idea of representing the objects as *being* the same. The sentences "Cicero = Tully" and "Cicero = Cicero" both represent the objects as being the same but only the second represents them as the same. And, in general, one cannot informatively represent objects as being the same compatibly with representing them as the same. A further difference is that only a single sentence (such as "Cicero = Tully") can represent its objects as being the same but two different sentences (e.g., "Cicero is Roman," "Cicero is an orator") can represent their objects as the same. Finally, what are in fact two distinct objects can be represented as being the same, as with the sentence "Cicero = Caesar." But two distinct objects cannot ever be represented as the same – or, at least, not without taking two names to be one or committing some other error of this kind.

However, to recognize the existence of same-as representation is not necessarily to endorse a relationist view; for other philosophers can acknowledge the phenomenon and yet give a nonrelational account of what it is. The relationist understanding of the phenomenon requires two further theses. The first is that the phenomenon is indeed semantic. When a piece of discourse represents an object as the same, then this is a semantic feature of the expressions by which reference to the object is made. The second is that the phenomenon is essentially relational; there are no intrinsic semantic features of the individual expressions in virtue of which they represent the object as the same.

Each of these further theses may be questioned. The advocates of "logical form" (among whom we may perhaps include Putnam (1954) and Kaplan (1990)) will argue that the phenomenon is pre-semantic. The difference between the pairs of names "Cicero", "Cicero" and "Cicero", "Tully," or between the identity sentences "Cicero = Cicero" and "Cicero = Tully," is one of logical form; and it is only once the logical form or "syntax" of the sentences has been determined that the question of semantics comes into play. The advocates of sense, on the other hand, will agree that the phenomenon is semantic but will take it simply to consist in the two names having the same or a different sense.

I believe that the first response is mistaken – or, at least, seriously off-track. For what is it for the logical form of "Cicero = Cicero" to be "a = a" rather than "a = b"? It cannot be a matter of having the same typographic name on the left and the right (whatever exactly that might be); for the name on the left could have been used for the orator and the name on the right for the spy. Nor can it be a matter of having the same name with the same reference on the left and the right (though this would be partly a semantic matter). For through a freak of transmigration, it might turn out that Cicero the orator is one and the same as Cicero the spy and, in this circumstance, the two uses of "Cicero" would still not represent the object as the same. Nor can it consist in the names themselves being the same. For what is it for the names in the relevant sense to be the same? As we have seen, it is not simply a matter of typographic identity or coreference. But then what else is required? Presumably that the names should represent the object *as* the same, which is just what we were after. We might also observe that in cases of anaphora (as when I say "I saw John, he was wearing a bowler hat"), we can have two expressions representing an object as the same without the expressions themselves being the same; and this suggests that there is some underlying phenomenon, not resting upon the expressions being the same, in virtue of which they represent the object *as* the same.

I would not wish to deny that the semantic relationship – of representing-as-the-same – might hold in virtue of a syntactic relationship – of the name being the same. It is, after all, a common occurrence that a semantic feature or relationship can hold in virtue of an underlying syntactic feature or relationship. It is, for example, because "snow is white" is a sentence that it is capable of being true or false and it is because "cats" is the plural of "cat" that it signifies "in the plural" what "cat" signifies "in the singular." But either the syntactic feature or relationship is constitutive of the supposedly semantic feature or relationship, in which case it is not genuinely semantic at all, or it is not constitutive of it, in which case there is a further semantic feature riding upon the syntax, whose exact nature needs to be ascertained.

The more serious challenge is from the advocate of sense. He agrees that the phenomenon is semantic but argues that when two names represent an object as the same it is because they represent the object in the same *way* and that the way in which an expression represents an object is none other than its sense. Now the relationist can agree that when two expressions represent an object as the same they represent the object in the same way. For, trivially, the second expression will represent the object the same as the second expression while, by assumption, the first expression will also represent the object the same as the second expression. However, he will deny that one can *account* for the expressions representing the object as the same in terms of *how* each represents its object. In other words, there is no intrinsic semantic feature of the expression, the way it represents its object, whose common possession accounts for the two expressions representing the object as the same.

This serves to undermine the intuitive basis for the sense-theorist's position. But, as we have already noted, the senses to which he wishes to appeal seem simply not to exist. In the previous Bruce case, for example, there appear to be no senses that might plausibly distinguish the two uses of the name and yet account for how each of the left uses and each of the right uses represent the object as the same. Senses, on this view, appear as the vestige of "ideas" under the old imagist theory of meaning; although they may have been drained of all mental content, they still function, in a ghostly manner, as intrinsic aspects of meaning.

So it looks as if the two alternatives to the relational view can be squashed. But still there is something unsatisfactory about the relational view. For if representing as the same is not a question of logical form or of a shared sense, then what is it? What other mechanism could possibly account for this peculiar form of representation?

C.   Semantic Fact

I would like to suggest that two expressions will represent an object as the same if it is a semantic fact that they represent the same object. Let us say that two names *strictly* corefer if it is a semantic fact that they corefer.[4] The suggestion is that for two names to represent an object as the same is for them strictly to corefer.

However, this suggestion calls for considerable clarification before it can be seen to be plausible. We should distinguish, in the first place, between facts that are semantic as to *topic* and semantic as to *status*. Certain properties and relations are, in a clear sense, semantic; they pertain to the meaning of the expressions to which they apply. *Truth*, for example, is a semantic property of sentences, *designation* a semantic relation between a term and an object, and *synonymy* a semantic relation between two expressions. A fact may be said to be *semantic* in the topic-oriented sense if it pertains to the exemplification of semantic properties or relations. Thus the fact that "the author of Waverley" designates Scott or that "bachelor" is synonymous with "unmarried man" will be semantic in this sense.

However, within the facts that are semantic as to topic, we may distinguish those that are also semantic as to status. These are the facts that are not merely statable in semantic terms but also belong to the semantics of a given language. Thus the fact that the sentence "snow is white" is true will not be semantic in this sense since it is not a fact about the semantics of English, while the synonymy of "bachelor" and "unmarried man" presumably will be.[5]

What does it take for a fact that is semantic as to topic also to be semantic as to status? A natural criterion, though not one altogether free of circularity, is that a fact semantic as to status will be wholly consequential upon the meaning of the expressions which it concerns, while one not semantic as to status will be partly consequential upon non-semantic considerations. Thus the truth of "snow is white" can be seen to be consequential upon the following two facts:

(i)   "snow is white" is true if snow is white;
(ii)   snow is white.

The first of these is purely semantic but the second is not; and, for this reason, the truth of "snow is white" will not be semantic as to status. On the other hand, there is no similar "factoring" of (i) and so its truth will be semantic as to status.[6] Our interest in what follows is in pure semantics; and so let us restrict the phrase "semantic fact" to the status-oriented conception.

We should, in the second place, distinguish between semantic *facts* and semantic *truths*. Semantic facts are *propositions*, or at least may be taken to be propositions, while semantic truths are *sentences*.[7] Thus the proposition that "Cicero" refers to the particular object Cicero is a semantic fact (at least for the referentialist), while the sentence "'Cicero' refers to Cicero" is a semantic truth. The semantic fact involves the name "Cicero," the particular object Cicero, and the relation of referring, while the semantic truth involves the quotation-mark name for "Cicero," the name "Cicero" itself, and the predicate "refers to."

In the same way, one should distinguish between a *semantics*, which is a body of semantic facts, and a *semantic theory*, which is a body of semantic truths. The whole point of what I subsequently say will be lost unless one keeps firmly in mind the distinction between semantics or semantic facts, on the one side, and semantic theory or semantic truths, on the other.

The natural view on the conceptual relationship between these various notions is as follows: semantic theory is to be understood in terms of semantic truth, a semantic theory being a body of semantic truths (perhaps satisfying some additional constraints); semantic truth is to be understood in terms of semantic fact, a semantic truth being a sentence that states a semantic fact (again, perhaps subject to some additional constraints). Current orthodoxy, deriving from Davidson (1967), reverses the natural conceptual order; semantic fact ("meaning") is to be understood in terms of semantic truth (or "theorem"); and semantic truth (or "theorem") is to be understood in terms of semantic theory. I consider this reversal of the natural order to be one of most unfortunate tendencies in contemporary philosophy of language. It is as if chemistry were to take itself to be concerned with chemical formulae rather than chemical facts, focusing on the language or theory by which the facts are stated rather than on the facts themselves. The slide between the two is more understandable when the facts themselves concern language but equally regrettable.

D.   Closure

There is one further, very significant, clarification in the notion of semantic fact that should be made. It may be introduced by means of a puzzle that appears to threaten the very notion of strict coreference.

To state the puzzle, we need the following two assumptions:

1   *Referentialism*. It is semantic fact that a proper name refers to the particular object that it does.
2   *Closure*. Logical consequences of semantic facts are semantic facts.

Let us now suppose that two names, say "Cicero" and "Tully," corefer. By Referentialism, it is a semantic fact that "Cicero" refers to a certain object and that "Tully" refers to that object; and so by Closure, it is a semantic fact that "Cicero" and "Tully" corefer. Thus coreference implies strict coreference; and clearly strict coreference implies coreference, since any semantic fact is a fact. The assumptions, therefore, lead to a collapse of the distinction between coreference and strict coreference. We should also note that even if we do not explain coordination as strict coreference, it is still puzzling, given this argument, what further semantic fact, beyond coreference, coordination might require.

If collapse is to be avoided, one of the two assumptions must be given up. But which? The Fregean, were he to consider the puzzle, would reject the referentialist assumption. For he would deny that it is *pure* semantic fact that "Cicero" referred to a particular object x. For the referentialist, on the other hand, the assumption is hardly negotiable. It is true that when it comes to a name whose reference is "fixed" by a description (as in Kripke (1980)), the referentialist *might* not take it to be a pure semantic fact that the name refers to what it does. But for a name whose reference is not fixed by a description, it surely will be a pure – and indeed a basic – semantic fact that the name refers to what it does.

So this leaves Closure. But how can this sensibly be doubted? How can the logical consequence of semantic facts fail to be semantic fact (perhaps setting aside those trivial cases in which the consequence is not itself semantic as to topic)?

All the same, I am inclined to think that it is Closure that should be relinquished. The issue is complicated by the circumstance that if there is a notion of semantic fact for which Closure fails then there will also be one for which it holds. For we may take a fact to be semantic *in the broad sense* if it is a logical consequence of the semantic facts in some original sense. Semantic facts in the broad sense will then conform to Closure by definition. Thus the issue is not whether there is a notion of semantic fact for which Closure holds, since there clearly is, but whether there is also one for which it fails.

The issue is further complicated by the circumstance that if there is a notion of semantic fact for which Closure holds then there is a notion of semantic fact – or, at least, of a quasi-semantic fact – for which it fails. For we may take a fact to be semantic *in this narrow sense* if it is a fact in the broad sense that is available to the speakers of the language. Semantic facts in this narrow sense will then fail to conform to Closure since a speaker may know that "Cicero" refers to a particular person and know that "Tully" refers to a particular person without being in a position to know that they are coreferential. Such a notion is of no use to the referentialist in solving Frege's puzzle since it fails to provide a genuinely semantic basis for distinguishing between the pairs "Cicero", "Cicero" and "Cicero", "Tully." Thus it is important not merely that there be some notion of semantic fact for which Closure fails but that it be a genuinely semantic notion and not simply a non-semantic restriction of the broader notion.

So the issue is delicate. But it seems to me that in so far as we have an independent understanding of the semantics facts, it is one for which Closure will fail. For the semantic facts, in this most basic sense, should be faithful to our intuitions of semantic difference; when intuitively there is a semantic difference between two languages, there should be a semantic fact in virtue of which this is so. But the broad notion is not faithful to these intuitions. This may be illustrated with an apocryphal story about Carl Hempel, the distinguished philosopher of science. When Hempel moved to Princeton, some of the philosophers there found the name "Carl" too Germanic for their taste and decided to use the English name "Peter" in its place. It is not that they *re-christened* Hempel with the name "Peter"; rather, they decided to use the name "Peter" as a *variant* of the name "Carl." Consider now a different scenario in which "Peter" is introduced, not as a variant of the name "Carl," but as a name in its own right: on arriving in Princeton, Hempel is re-christened "Peter" (perhaps even in ignorance of his German name). For the referential-ist, the semantic facts in the broad sense for the two languages or idiolects are the same; "Peter" refers to Hempel, "Carl" refers to Hempel, and that is it. But intuitively, there is a semantic difference between the two languages, since it is a *convention* of the first language, though not of the second, that the name "Peter" should be coreferential with "Carl." Someone who had competency in the use of each name but failed to recognize that the two names were coreferential would thereby display his lack of understanding of the first language, though not of the second.[8] For a narrow notion of semantic fact, on the other hand, the semantic facts for the two languages are not the same since in one it is a semantic fact that "Peter" and "Carl" refer, though not in the other. It is not that the semantics of the two languages are the same and that there is a difference in the speaker's access to these facts, the facts themselves are different; and this suggests that it is the semantic facts in the narrower sense which come first and that semantics, more broadly conceived, has no independent status except as the closure or "rounding out" of semantics more narrowly conceived.

However, if the present proposal is to be sustained, there are two important objections to it that must be met. The first is that it is unmotivated. The rejection of Closure may save us from certain awkward consequences; but one would like to have some independent reason for thinking that the notion of semantic fact is one for which Closure should fail. The second is that it is unwork-able. For the compositional character of semantics requires that we should derive semantic facts concerning complex expressions from the semantic facts concerning simpler expressions. And how is this possible unless the notion of semantic fact is subject to Closure?

I believe that the response to the first objection turns upon more general questions concerning the possibility of inferential knowledge; and so let us consider these before considering how they might apply to the specific case of semantics. Imagine an ideal cognitive agent, one who is perfectly competent in drawing inferences from what he knows. One then naturally assumes that he will know (or be in a position to know) every classical consequence of what he knows. But this is not something that the referentialist should grant, at least when singular propositions are in question. For our ideal cognizer may know that the object x Fs under one "take" on x and that x Gs under another "take" on x, but not be in a position to infer that x both Fs and Gs, or even that *something* both Fs and Gs. He may know, for example, that Paderewski is a brilliant pianist (having heard him at a concert) and also that he is a charismatic statesman (having observed him at a political rally), without realizing that it is the same person who is both.[9] Since x's being both F and G (or something's being F and G) is a classical consequence of x's being F and x's being G, the referentialist cannot take knowledge, even for an ideal cognizer, to be closed under classical consequence.

However, the knowledge of the ideal cognizer is far from being logically inert, even when singular propositions are in question. From the fact that x Fs, for example, he may infer that something Fs; and from the fact that every F Gs and x Fs, he may infer that x Gs. Let us say that a given proposition q is a *manifest* consequence of other propositions $p_1, p_2, p_3, \ldots$ if it is a classical consequence of them and if, in addition, it would be manifest to any ideal cognizer who knew the propositions $p_1, p_2, p_3, \ldots$ that q was indeed a classical consequence of those propositions. In other words, the ideal cognizer would not be handicapped by his different "takes" on the objects occurring in the premises $p_1, p_2, p_3, \ldots$ in recognizing that the conclusion q was a consequence of them. Knowledge of the ideal cognizer would then be closed under manifest consequence, even if not under classical consequence.[10]

We might give a more formal definition of manifest consequence as follows. Say that p' is a *differentiation of* the proposition p if it is the result of replacing distinct occurrences of the same object by distinct objects (this corresponds to the possibility that even though the objects are in fact the same they may not appear to be the same to the cognizer). The proposition q will then be a manifest consequence of the propositions $p_1, p_2, p_3, \ldots$ if, for any differentiation $p_1', p_2', p_3', \ldots$ of $p_1, p_2, p_3, \ldots$, there is a differentiation q' of q for which q' is a classical consequence of $p_1', p_2', p_3', \ldots$.[11]

So, for example, the inference from propositions of the form Fa and Ga to the proposition $\exists x(Fx \ \& \ Gx)$ will not be manifestly valid. For if we differentiate the premises into Fa' and Ga", the corresponding inference from Fa' and Ga" to $\exists x(Fx \ \& \ Gx)$ (here no differentiation of the conclusion is possible) will not be classically valid. On the other hand, the inference from Fa and Ga to Fa & Ga *will* be manifestly valid. For take any differentiation Fa', Ga'' of the premises, then the inference from the differentiated premises Fa', Ga'' to the correspondingly differentiated conclusion Fa' & Ga'' will be classically valid.

Corresponding to this distinction between classical and manifest consequence is a distinction between two kinds of *domain*. Just as a theory may be taken to be a class of sentences closed under consequence, so we may take a domain to be a class of *propositions* that is closed under consequence. We then have two kinds of domain, depending upon whether consequence is taken to be classical or manifest. These two kinds of domain correspond to two kinds of attitudes one might have towards their content. On the one hand, one might regard the domain as a possible domain of *facts*. It is then only natural that it should be taken to be closed under classical consequence since the classical consequences of facts are also facts. On the other hand, one might think of the domain as a possible domain of *information*; it consists of what one might know rather than what might be true. It is then only natural that it should be taken to be closed under manifest – rather than classical – consequence, since it is only the manifest consequences of known facts that need be known.

How these general considerations apply to the case of semantics depends upon whether one regards semantics as a body of fact, something to be "found" in the world, or as a body of information, something to be "found" in the mind of the speaker. In the former case, it should be closed under classical consequence while, in the latter case, it should, at best, only be closed under manifest consequence. Now there is a tradition in the philosophy of language which sees the semantics of a given language as a body of knowledge that is somehow implicit in the speaker's use of the language. It is not that he must explicitly know the semantics or consciously apply it but it must at least be possible to see his use of the language as being in conformity with his hypothetical possession of this knowledge. Given this view, one would then expect the semantics for his language to be behave like an informational rather than a factual domain and to be closed under manifest rather than classical consequence.

Under this conception of semantics, we can now easily take care of the two objections. Coreference will not imply strict coreference since the fact that two names corefer is only a classical not a manifest consequence of the fact that each refers to what it does. Also, Compositionality can be respected. For an examination of how Compositionality is used in developing a semantics will show that appeal never need be made to classical as opposed to manifest consequence. The fact that "Cicero" and "Tully" are coreferential, for example, is irrelevant to developing the semantics for sentences containing these names. All that we need know is that "Cicero" refers to x and that "Tully" refers to x. The semantic value of expressions containing these names can then be determined in the usual way; and there is never any need to make use of the information that the two names refer to the same thing.

We might talk of semantic "requirements," or of what is semantically "required," when the narrow conception is in question and talk of "semantic facts" when the broad or neutral conception is in question. Thus semantics, as we are conceiving it, is given by a body of semantic requirements rather than semantic facts; and it is in terms of these requirements rather than the facts themselves that the notion of strict coreference is to be understood.

The present conception of semantics as a domain of requirements is broadly Kantian in spirit. For what we have in the distinction between a body of semantic requirements and a body of semantic facts is an instance of a more general distinction between a domain that is subjectively given (the phenomena) and a corresponding domain that is objective (the noumena). Given two such domains, there arises the question of priority. Should we understand what is subjectively given as some kind of "internalization" of what is objective, with an understanding of the objective coming first, or should we understand what is objective as some kind of "externalization" of what is subjectively given, with an understanding of what is subjectively given coming first. The broadly Kantian view gives priority to the subjective; and this is in line with our thinking in the present case. For rather than regarding the subjectively given semantics as the accessible portion of the objective semantics, we take the objective semantics to be an inaccessible "rounding out" or closure of the subjectively given semantics.

E.   Referentialism Reconsidered

With the requisite notion of strict coreference in place, let us review the argument to date and consider some of its implications for the doctrine of referentialism.

According to the abridged version of Frege's puzzle, there is a semantic difference between the identity sentences "Cicero = Cicero" and "Cicero = Tully." But there can be no semantic difference between the sentences without a semantic difference between the names "Cicero" and "Tully" and there can be no semantic difference between the names without a referential difference. And yet there is no referential difference! The last assumption (no referential difference) is not reasonably open to doubt and so one of the other three assumptions must be given up. Fregeans give up the third assumption; they maintain that a semantic difference between two names is compatible with there being no referential difference. Referentialists give up the first assumption; they maintain that there is no semantic difference between the two identity sentences.

I have suggested that, in analogy with the corresponding puzzle for variables, one should give up neither the first nor the third assumptions, but the second. A semantic difference between the identity sentences only strictly implies a semantic difference between the *pairs* of names "Cicero", "Cicero" and "Cicero", "Tully" but we may deny that semantic difference between the pairs of names need imply a semantic difference between the names themselves. There may, in other words, be a semantic relationship between "Cicero" and "Cicero" that does not hold between "Cicero" and "Tully," despite the lack of an intrinsic semantic difference between the names themselves.

This proposal gave rise to the difficulty of saying what the alleged semantic relationship actually is. I suggested that it was the relationship that held between two names when they *strictly* coreferred, i.e. when it was semantically required that their reference should be the same. We may then maintain that "Cicero" is strictly coreferential with "Cicero" but that "Cicero" is only accidentally (not strictly) coreferential with "Tully." However, if this way of drawing the distinction is to be viable, we must conceive of semantics as a body of semantic requirements rather than facts and as closed under manifest rather than classical consequence.

As the reader is no doubt aware, I have only considered Frege's original form of the puzzle, in which the critical sentences involve two name-occurrences apiece. But the puzzle also arises for the case of a single name-occurrence, as with the sentences "Cicero is an orator" and "Tully is an orator." Given that these sentences are semantically or cognitively different, a puzzle can then be generated in the same way as before.

It is commonly supposed that the two versions of the puzzle call for a common solution. But the relationalist's response to the monadic version of the puzzle must be somewhat different from his response to the dyadic version, for he can no longer maintain that there is an intrinsic semantic difference between the sentences "Cicero is an orator" and "Tully is an orator" (just as he cannot maintain that there is an intrinsic semantic difference between the open-sentences "x is an orator" and "y is an orator"). He can, however, appeal to a *relative* difference between the two sentences, that is, a difference in the semantic relationship that each of them bears to other sentences, and to a corresponding relative difference between the two names. For the first sentence will be strictly equivalent with the sentence "Cicero is an orator" – it will be semantically required that they have the same truth-value or express the same uncoordinated proposition – while the second sentence will not be; and, again, the name "Cicero" will be strictly coreferential with "Cicero," while the name "Tully" is not. As David Kaplan has put it to me, we may obtain the difference through "triangulation."

It might be thought to be an embarrassment for the relationist that he does not take there to be an intrinsic semantic difference between the sentences or the names in this case, for does there not appear to be such a difference? I am unsure what to make of our intuitions on this score. It seems clear that there is a semantic difference between the sentences "Cicero is an orator" and "Tully is an orator"; and it also seems clear that there is an intrinsic semantic difference between the sentences "Cicero = Cicero" and "Cicero = Tully" or between the pairs of names "Cicero", "Cicero" and "Cicero", "Tully." But it is not so clear that there is an *intrinsic* semantic difference between the sentences "Cicero is an orator" and "Tully is an orator" or between the individual names "Cicero" and "Tully." One is perhaps tempted to think that there is an intrinsic semantic difference between the two sentences because one associates different information with the two names and then takes this difference in information to reflect a semantic difference. But consider a case in which a speaker associates the very same information with the two names (perhaps "famous Roman orator"). There would then appear to be no intrinsic semantic mark by which the two names or the two sentences might be distinguished. There is, of course, a cognitive difference between the two sentences but it should not automatically be assumed that this requires an intrinsic semantic difference; and, indeed, we shall argue in chapter 3 (section D) that a cognitive difference is compatible with there being only a relative semantic difference between the two sentences.

Millianism is the application of referentialism to names. It holds that the meaning, or semantic function, of a name is entirely given by what it refers to. The doctrine, therefore, has a positive and a negative part. According to the positive part, it is at least part of the semantic function of a name to refer to a particular bearer; and according to the negative part, there is no more to the semantic function of a name.

A relationist view of names is compatible with the positive doctrine and naturally goes with it. Whether it is compatible with the negative doctrine depends upon what exactly it is taken to state.[12] If it states merely that there is no more to the intrinsic semantic function of a name than what it refers to, then it may well be accepted by the relationist. But if it is taken to state that there is no more to the semantic function of the name *all told*, then it must be rejected, since there will be relational aspects to the meaning of names that do not simply follow from the intrinsic aspects of their meaning.

F.   A Relational Semantics for Names

There is a standard referentialist semantics for a language containing names. The semantic value, or content, of a name is the object that it refers to, the content of a predicate is a property, and the content of a logical connective is an operation on propositions (for present purposes, we may ignore the quantifiers and intensional operators such as "know" or "believes"). The content of complex expressions is then determined in familiar compositional fashion from the contents of the simpler expressions from which it is formed. Thus, given that the content of "Cicero" is a certain object and the content of "is an orator" a certain property, the content of the sentence "Cicero is an orator" will be a proposition to the effect that the object has the property.

The most distinctive feature of the semantics is that the propositions assigned to sentences containing names are *singular*; where the names refer to certain individuals, the propositions will involve those very individuals without regard for how they might be "given." In developing a rigorous account of the semantics, there are somewhat different conceptions of a singular proposition that one might adopt. However, the choice between them will not be important for our purposes. All that matters is that we should be able to talk meaningfully of the *occurrences* of an individual in a proposition and that we should be able to talk meaningfully of *substituting* one individual for the occurrence of another within a given proposition. Thus it should make sense to say that the singular proposition that Cicero is an orator contains one occurrence of Cicero and that the singular proposition that Cicero is identical to Cicero contains two occurrences; and it should also make sense to say that the singular proposition that Bush is an orator is the result of substituting Bush for Cicero in the proposition that Cicero is an orator.[13]

The standard referentialist semantics ignores semantic relationships. Each occurrence of a name within an expression puts an individual into its content; and it makes no difference to the content whether two names within the expression are strictly or accidentally coreferential. Thus "Cicero loves Cicero" and "Cicero loves Tully" will each be assigned the same content.

Let us now show how to develop a semantics that is able to take account of semantic relationships; differences in semantic relationship between names will actually show up as differences in content (the extension to other parts of speech will be considered later).

The natural way to proceed is to let differences in "coordination" among names show up as differences in coordination among the objects to which they correspond. Consider again the sentences "Cicero loves Cicero" and "Cicero loves Tully." They express the same singular proposition, one to the effect that a given individual, Cicero, loves Cicero. The proposition in question will, therefore, contain two occurrences of the individual Cicero. But, in the proposition expressed by the first sentence, the two occurrences of Cicero should be taken to be coordinated, thereby indicating that they are

Figure 2.1   Proposition 1

Figure 2.2   Proposition 2

represented as the same, whereas in the proposition expressed by the second sentence, they should be taken to be uncoordinated, thereby indicating that they are not represented as the same. Thus we might depict the first proposition by Figure 2.1, which has a connected upper line to represent the coordination between the two occurrences of Cicero. And we might depict the second proposition by Figure 2.2, which has an annulled upper line to represent the lack of coordination between the two occurrences of Cicero.

Just as there may be coordination (or lack of it) within a proposition, so there may be coordination (or lack of it) across propositions or other kinds of content. Consider the sentence-pairs "Cicero is Roman", "Cicero is an orator" and "Cicero is Roman", "Tully is an orator." Each pair of sentences expresses the same pair of singular propositions. But there is a semantic difference between the two pairs, since the subject-terms are strictly coreferential in the first pair, though not in the second. If we are to reflect this difference at the level of content, we should require that the (identical) subjects of the propositions be coordinated in the first case but not in the second.

The general notion of propositional coordination might be defined as follows, in obvious analogy to the earlier syntactic notion of coordination for variables (chapter 1, section G). Suppose we are given a sequence of propositions (or contents) $P = p_1, p_2, \ldots, p_n$ ($n > 0$). By a *coordination-scheme* $\mathcal{C}$ *for* P is meant an equivalence relation on the occurrences of individuals in $p_1, p_2 \ldots, p_n$ which is such that two occurrences of individuals are related by $\mathcal{C}$ only if they are occurrences of the same individual. Intuitively, a coordination-scheme tells us how the occurrences of individuals within the propositions are or are not coordinated. A *coordinated sequence of* propositions (or contents) is then an ordered pair $(P; \mathcal{C})$ where P is a sequence of propositions (or contents) and $\mathcal{C}$ is a coordination-scheme for P.

Suppose, for example, that p is the single (uncoordinated) proposition to the effect that Cicero loves Cicero and that c_1 and c_2 are the two occurrences of Cicero in p. There are then two coordination-schemes for p: one, call it $\mathcal{C}_1$, relating c_1 to c_2; and the other, call it $\mathcal{C}_2$, *not* relating c_1 to c_2. The schemes $\mathcal{C}_1$ and $\mathcal{C}_2$ give rise to two corresponding coordinated propositions, $p^+ = (p; \mathcal{C}_1)$ and $p^- = (p; \mathcal{C}_2)$, where the occurrences c_1 and c_2 of Cicero are (*positively*) coordinated in p^+ and *negatively* coordinated in p^-. We should, of course, distinguish the negatively coordinated proposition $p^- = (p; \mathcal{C}_2)$ from the plain uncoordinated proposition p, since p contains no specification – either positive or negative – as to how the occurrences of Cicero are to be coordinated.[14]

Sometimes we shall not be interested in the given ordering $P = p_1$, $p_2, \ldots, p_n$ of the propositions in the coordinated sequence $(P; \mathcal{C})$. Now each reordering P' of $p_1, p_2, \ldots, p_n$ (say as $p_n, p_2, p_1, p_3 \ldots, p_{n-1}$) will give rise to a corresponding coordinated sequence $(P'; \mathcal{C}')$ in which the original coordination-scheme $\mathcal{C}$ is readjusted to match the reordering of the original ordering P. We may then take a coordinated *body of* propositions to be a set of coordinated sequences of propositions, consisting of a given coordinated sequence $(P; \mathcal{C})$ and all of the corresponding coordinated sequences $(P'; \mathcal{C}')$. In this way, we may abstract from the ordering in the given coordinated sequence. We should note that a coordinated body of propositions is capable of containing several different occurrences of the same proposition. $P = p_1, p_2$, for example, may consist of two occurrences of the proposition that Cicero is an orator (corresponding to the sentences "Cicero is an orator" and "Tully is an orator"), with neither occurrence of Cicero positively coordinated to the other.[15]

A compositional semantics for assigning coordinated content to the expressions of our language may now be given, again in rough analogy to the previous relational semantics for variables. To the pair of names "Cicero", "Cicero," for example, will be assigned the positively coordinated sequence of individuals Cicero, Cicero (the coordination-scheme will relate each occurrence of Cicero to the other) while, to the pair of names "Cicero", "Tully," will be assigned the negatively coordinated sequence of individuals Cicero, Cicero (the coordination-scheme will fail to relate each occurrence of Cicero to the other). The coordinated propositions assigned to "Cicero = Cicero" and "Cicero = Tully" can then be determined in the obvious manner on the basis of the content of "=" and the coordinated sequence of individuals assigned either to "Cicero", "Cicero" or to "Cicero", "Tully" (where the occurrences of Cicero in the coordinated proposition assigned to the identity sentence will be positively or negatively coordinated according as to whether the occurrences of Cicero in the content of the corresponding pairs of names are positively or negatively coordinated). Similarly, to the pair of sentences "Cicero is a Roman", "Cicero is an orator," will be assigned the positively coordinated sequence of propositions *Cicero is a Roman*, *Cicero is an orator* while, to the pair of sentences "Cicero is a Roman" and "Tully is an orator," will be assigned the negatively coordinated sequence of the same propositions. The coordinated propositions assigned to the conjunctions "Cicero is a Roman and Cicero is an orator" and "Cicero is a Roman and Tully is an orator" can then be determined, in a similar way, on the basis of the coordinated sequences of propositions assigned to the respective sequences of their conjuncts. Following through this suggestion in a systematic way, a relational semantic for a language containing names can then be obtained.

It may be helpful, in concluding this section, to draw some comparisons between the familiar referential semantics for names, the Fregean semantics for names, and our own relational semantics. The familiar referentialist semantics is one-tier; there is merely one level of semantic value and one level of semantic evaluation at which it is computed. This is in contrast to the familiar Fregean semantics, under which semantic value can be computed at the level both of reference and of sense. In this respect, our relational semantics is closer to the Fregean semantics than to the familiar referential semantics, since it provides a method of computing semantic value at the level both of uncoordinated and of coordinated content.

However, the parallel between them is not at all exact and it will be worth spelling out some of the similarities and differences. To this end, let us use the term "primary content" for reference under the Fregean semantics and for uncoordinated content under the relational semantics and let us use the term "secondary content" for sense under the Fregean semantics and for coordinated content under the relational semantics. Then in both cases, the primary and secondary content of a complex expression will each be compositionally determined on the basis of the primary and secondary content of simpler expressions. In both cases, secondary content will be determinative of primary content; it will be possible to read off the reference of an expression from its sense and the uncoordinated content of an expression from its coordinated content; and just as expressions with the same reference may differ in their sense, so may expressions with the same uncoordinated content differ in their coordinated content. Finally, the secondary content, in both cases, can be regarded as the way in which we grasp the primary content; we grasp the reference of an expression through its sense and the uncoordinated content through its coordinated content.

However, there are also some significant differences between the two cases. First, the determination of sense, under the Fregean semantics, runs strictly parallel to the determination of reference, each being based upon the very same syntactic analysis of the expression under consideration. But the determination of coordinated content, under the relational semantics, does not run parallel to the determination of uncoordinated content, for the former proceeds along standard intrinsicalist lines, in accordance with the usual syntactic analysis, whereas the latter works off the semantic connections between component expressions.

Second, under the Fregean account, sense and reference stand in an external relationship; the sense is genuinely determinative of the reference and it is, in general, a contingent matter that the sense has a given referent. Under the relationist account, by contrast, coordinated and uncoordinated content stand in an internal relationship; the non-coordinated content is "built into" the coordinated content and it is impossible for a given coordinated content to be associated with a different uncoordinated content.

Third, sense is not a relational matter. It is to be assigned to single expressions, one at a time, and the only meaning we can give to the sense of several expressions is in terms of the sense that is given to each individual expression. Coordination, on the other hand, *is* a relational matter. Coordinated content may be assigned to several expressions, considered together, and it is not, in general, a function of the coordinated content of each expression.

Fourth, the sense of a sentence is descriptive or truth-conditional in character; it bears upon the conditions under which the sentence is true (and, in general, the sense of an expression will bear upon the conditions under which it has application to the world). But the coordinative aspect of the coordinated content of a sentence, such as "Cicero killed Cicero," is entirely lacking in any special descriptive or truth-conditional character and relates entirely to how its truth-conditions (Cicero's suicide) are to be grasped. It is a significant feature of the traditional Fregean view that there can be no difference in what it is to grasp the sense of an expression without there being a difference in how the sense has application to the world. Suppose, for example, that we understand "Hesperus" as *the evening star* and "Phosphorus" as *the morning star*. Then this difference in sense corresponds to a difference in what it takes for the sentences "Hesperus is visible" and "Phosphorus is visible" to be true. But under the relational view, these two aspects of sense come completely apart. There is no difference in what it takes for the sentences "Cicero wrote about Cicero" and "Cicero wrote about Tully" to be true, even though there is a difference in their coordinated content.

It might be wondered how there can be such elusive differences in meaning. But what it comes down to, in the end, is a difference in the content of semantic requirements. In saying that "Cicero = Cicero" expresses the positively coordinated proposition that $c = c$, what I am saying is that it is a semantic requirement that the sentence signifies an identity proposition whose subject and object positions are both occupied by the object c while, in saying that "Cicero = Tully" expresses the uncoordinated proposition that $c = c$, I am merely saying that it is a semantic requirement that it signifies an identity proposition whose subject position is occupied by c and whose object position is occupied by c. Under classical consequence, the contents of the two requirements are equivalent. But under manifest consequence they are not and the requirements are, therefore, capable of reflecting a genuine difference in meaning.

Finally, and most significantly, sense is much more varied than coordinated content. There is only one coordinated proposition corresponding to the uncoordinated proposition that Cicero is an orator and only two coordinated propositions corresponding to the uncoordinated proposition that Cicero admires Cicero (depending upon whether or not the two occurrences of Cicero are linked). But there will be a multitude of senses corresponding to any given referent and hence a multitude of propositions that might be expressed in the form "Cicero is an orator," differing only in the sense that is to be attached to "Cicero." Coordination does the work, not of sense, but of sameness of sense; and any variation in how sameness of sense might be realized is not something that it can capture.

G.   Transparency

It is often supposed that referentialism is incompatible with the "transparency" or "accessibility" of meaning. My aim in this section is to make clear how this conflict arises (using a variant of Frege's puzzle) and then to show how the distinction between semantic facts and requirements enables the referentialist to evade the conflict. Thus relationism not only enables the referentialist to account for the non-triviality of identity sentences; it also enables him to hang on to the transparency of meaning.

For present purposes, it will be helpful to work with a reasonably precise notion of accessibility. So let us say that a fact concerning a given language, or portion of a language, L is *accessible to the understanding* if any rational and reflective individual who understands L is thereby in a position to know that the fact obtains. For example: anyone who understands the expressions "bachelor" and "unmarried man" is in a position to know that they are synonymous; and anyone who understands the sentence "snow is white" is in a position to know that "snow is white" is true if and only if snow is white. These facts of synonymy and of equivalence are, therefore, accessible to the understanding in the sense I have in mind.

In saying that the cognizer would be in a *position* to know, I mean that he actually would know as long as nothing short of further empirical knowledge stands in the way of his knowing. He gives the matter some thought, the right questions are put to him, he is not confused, etc.; and, of course, he should be allowed to have whatever concepts are required to reflect on his own use of the language.

We may now bring out the conflict between Closure and Transparency by enlarging upon the previous puzzle concerning strict coreference. The new puzzle is based upon the two previous assumptions, Referentialism and Closure, and three additional assumptions.[16]

- Principles:
  1 *Referentialism*. It is a semantic fact that a proper name refers to the particular object that it does.
  2 *Closure*. Logical consequences of semantic facts are semantic facts.
  3 *Transparency*. Semantic facts are accessible to the understanding.
- Data:
  4 *Cognitive Datum*. The fact that "Cicero" and "Tully" corefer is not accessible to the understanding.
  5 *Semantic Datum*. The proper names "Cicero" and "Tully" corefer.

The five assumptions are jointly inconsistent. For we have already seen that Semantic Datum, Referentialism and Closure imply that it is a semantic fact that "Cicero" and "Tully" corefer. But then by Transparency, it follows that their coreferentiality is accessible to the understanding – contrary to Cognitive Datum.[17]

So which of the assumptions should be given up? I assume that the data are beyond reasonable doubt. Certainly, "Cicero" and "Tully" (in their most familiar use) corefer. But it also seems evident that a competent user of a language which contains those two names need not be in a position to know that they corefer. If he subsequently learns that they do, he thereby adds to his knowledge of Roman lore, not to his understanding of the language.

This leaves the three principles – Referentialism, Transparency and Closure. As I have mentioned, the referentialist will surely accept Referentialism; and so only Transparency and Closure remain. Thus the puzzle reveals a conflict between Transparency and Closure; granted Referentialism, one or the other must be given up. Most (if not all) referentialists have been inclined to reject Transparency. Indeed, it is often taken to be one of the principal lessons of referentialism that the connection between understanding and semantic knowledge – as embodied in the doctrine of transparency – should be severed.

I think that part of what has made this seem plausible is the confusion of Transparency, as we have stated it, with some closely related theses. Thus Transparency is often stated in the form: the fact that two expressions mean the same is accessible to the understanding.

Now we may grant that it is a semantic requirement that an expression means what it does and hence is accessible to the understanding. But if Closure fails, then there is no reason to suppose that it is a semantic requirement that two expressions should mean the same and hence also be accessible to the understanding.[18] We, therefore, see that once Transparency is properly formulated, the supposed conflict with referentialism can be avoided.

It also seems to me that Transparency is independently plausible, although not for the reasons that have sometimes been given. Thus it is sometimes claimed that Transparency will follow from a proper conception of what it is to understand a language; for our understanding of a language, it is argued, will consist – wholly or in part – in our implicit knowledge of the semantic facts by which it is governed. However, it is not at all evident that we should give an account of our understanding of language along these lines; and such an account is especially problematic for the referentialist as opposed to the Fregean. For consider our "understanding" of a proper name, such as "Cicero." The suggestion is that this should be taken to consist in our knowledge that "Cicero" refers to Cicero. But when we acquire the use of the name from another speaker, this knowledge is itself most plausibly taken to derive from our understanding of the name, rather than the other way round.[19]

The truth of Transparency is more plausibly taken to follow, not from what is involved in our understanding a language, but from what is involved in our using a language that is already understood. To take but one example (there are many others): we may learn from what others tell us. You say "Cicero is an orator" and, being an ignoramus about Roman history, I thereby learn that Cicero is an orator. But how? The natural explanation is this. Through listening to what you say, I learn that the sentence is true (I do not have any immediate access to its content); but I already know that the sentence is true only if Cicero is an orator and hence am able to infer that Cicero is an orator. But this account requires that I already know the semantic fact that "Cicero is an orator" is true only if Cicero is an orator. It is plausible that our knowledge of other particular semantic facts might be justified in a similar way. And given our knowledge of the particular semantic facts, this is then plausibly taken to derive from our knowledge of the general semantic facts (in much the same way in which our knowledge of particular arithmetical facts is plausibly taken to derive from our knowledge of general arithmetical facts).[20]

Here, then, is a defense of Transparency that should appeal to referentialists and Fregeans alike. It is not required that semantic knowledge be *constitutive* of understanding but that it should at least be *consequential* upon our understanding, since it is otherwise a mystery how we might make the kind of use of language that we do.[21]

There is also another line of argument that might be developed in favor of some form of transparency, even when considerations of "use" or "understanding" are put to one side. Suppose Transparency were to fail (for the notion of semantic fact of interest to semantics). This would then appear to give rise to two serious methodological problems. The first is this: how are we to determine the proper domain of semantics? How, in other words, are we to determine, from all the facts which are semantic as to topic, those which are semantic as to status – or *pure*? Why, for example, should the referentialist not maintain that it is a pure semantic fact that "Cicero" refers to a famous Roman orator? The referentialist who believes in Transparency can appeal to the fact that someone may have the use of the name and yet not know that it refers to a famous Roman orator (and similarly for the linguistic community at large). But this line of argument is not open to the referentialist who rejects Transparency and, in its absence, it is hard to see how the question might reasonably be settled. The second problem is this. Understanding of a language, it is supposed, does not require knowledge of all of the semantic facts by which it is governed; and yet clearly, it requires knowledge of some of these semantic facts. But which? Again, there appears to be no reasonable basis upon which the question might be answered.

An analogy with the case of chess may help to bring the point home. Imagine a philosopher – call him an "occultist" – who rejects the counterpart of transparency for chess. He holds that someone who knows how to play chess may not thereby be in a position to know the rules by which it is governed. This philosopher then faces analogues of the problems posed above. First, what determines whether something is a rule of chess? Suppose in fact that no game has involved, or will ever involve, a certain sequence of moves. Then on what basis do we say that it is not a rule of chess that such a sequence of moves is forbidden? We cannot appeal to what the chess players take to be the rules, since we have conceded that there are rules of which they may be unaware. But then how else is the question to be settled? Second, it is clear that the ability to play chess depends upon knowing some of the rules. But which? Again, there would appear to be no reasonable basis upon which the question might be answered. The view that there are occult rules of chess is absurd on its face. The view that there are occult rules of language may not be evidently absurd but it is subject to similar difficulties, all the same.

Once we endorse Transparency, these various difficulties disappear. There is no problem of demarcating pure semantics, since the knowledge of the competent speaker provides a reasonable test of what is pure; and there is no problem of determining which of the semantic facts must be knowable in order to understand the language, since *all* of them must be knowable. The adherent of Transparency faces a single, well-conceived project – to determine the pure semantic facts: his opponent, by contrast, faces two ill-conceived projects – to separate the pure semantic facts from those that are impure and to determine which of the pure facts are essential for understanding.

The distinctive way in which we have endorsed Transparency enables us to steer a middle course between a conception of semantics that is either unduly objective or unduly subjective. As has often been observed, language is Janus-faced. In the one direction, it faces out towards to the world; it represents the various things in the world and how they might be related. In the other direction, language faces in towards to the speaker; it is something which the speaker can understand or "grasp" and thereby make his own.

Different approaches to the philosophy of language have tended to give primacy to one of these aspects of language over the other. The Fregean emphasizes the orientation towards the speaker. What makes language meaningful is its possession of sense; and it is this which the speaker grasps in understanding the language and *through* which the language relates to the world. The referentialist, on the other hand, emphasizes the orientation of language towards the world. What makes language meaningful are its representational relationships; and it is through these that it will relate to the world. It is not so clear on this view what it is to grasp a language but it will not in general be true that the meaning of a language, as given by its representational relationships, is something that the speakers of the language can directly grasp. Thus on the one view, the meaning of a language will be accessible to the speakers of the language though not in a way that allows it to relate directly to the world while, on the other view, language will relate directly to the world though not in a way that allows its meaning to be directly accessible to the speakers of the language.

Our own view also takes the meaning of language to be given by its representational relationship to the world but our conception of what these representational relationships are is circumscribed in such a way that the meaning of the language will in general be accessible to its speakers. We thereby make the same component of language responsible both for its external relationship to the world and for its internal embodiment within the speaker. Of course, the internalization is not achieved through purely internal mental states; in understanding a name, for example, the speaker must be appropriately related to the bearer. But given that the speaker understands the language – something that is not itself a purely internal matter – he will then be in a position to know what his language means.

What I previously called the Kantian point of view is able, in this way, to provide an integrated framework within which language might be directly oriented towards both the speaker and the world.

Chapter 3
Coordination within Thought

I have so far been concerned with the relational aspects of representation within language. I now wish to turn to their presence within
thought; and I shall argue that, just as there are semantical relationships between expressions that are not to be understood in terms of
their intrinsic semantical features, so there are representational relationships between the constituents of thought that are not to be
understood in terms of intrinsic representational features. If this is
right, then it means that the apparatus of coordinated content is
equally applicable within the realm of thought – to belief, knowledge,
intention, and the like – as it is within the realm of language.

I begin by considering standard accounts of coordination within
thought and argue that they are inadequate (section A). I then develop
a relational alternative – one in which coordination within thought
is taken to be a form of strict co-representation, in analogy to our
previous account of coordination within language as a form of strict
coreference (section B). Finally, I consider two further versions of
Frege's puzzle, which appear to show that sense is required at the
level of thought if not at language. For how can the thought that
Cicero is an orator be different from the thought that Tully is an
orator and how can the sentences "Cicero is an orator" and "Tully
is an orator" convey different information unless Cicero is somehow
associated with different senses or modes of presentation? I believe
that it is only by going relational that these puzzles can be satisfac-
torily solved within a referentialist framework, for it is only in this
way that we can respect the difference in the thoughts or in the information conveyed without either invoking sense or postulating a fundamental difference in the representational character of language and
of thought (sections C and D).

A.   Intentional Coordination

I previously maintained that there was an intuitive notion of two names semantically representing an object as the same. It seems to me that there is a similar intuitive notion of a thought, or thoughts, intentionally representing an object as the same. Suppose you try to recall what you know about Cicero. You think: *he is a Roman*; and you also think: *he is an orator* (of course, you don't necessarily think these thoughts in those very words or in words at all). Your two thoughts then represent the object, Cicero, as the same.

Coordination of this sort is, I believe, a pervasive aspect of our mental life. Suppose, for example, that I continuously observe an object – say a snake. I first see it coiled and later see it uncoil. The various momentary observations that make up the continuous observation then all represent the snake as the same. It is not like seeing a snake on two separate occasions and judging that it is the same. Here the series of observations actually represents the snake as the same from one moment to the next; and if the snake is not in fact the same (through some clever substitution, say), then one has suffered from a peculiar form of perceptual illusion. The same is also true of other forms of "sustained" representation – as when I recall a particular object or event or keep some object in mind.

But what is it to represent an object as the same within one's thought? Many philosophers might be tempted nowadays to explain the phenomenon in terms of "mental files." It is supposed that we keep mental files of every object of which we are capable of having singular thoughts. To coordinate, or represent an object as the same from one occasion to the next, is then to associate it with the same mental file. Thus in the example above, the two thoughts will associate the object Cicero with the same mental file and will thereby represent the object as the same.

It is hard to know what to make of this suggestion since it is hard to know what talk of mental files is meant to convey. Perhaps one thing it may reasonably be taken to convey is that certain items of information are *stored* together in a single "location," while other items of information are not. Thus the information that Cicero is a Roman and that Cicero is an orator will be stored in the same location, while the information that Cicero is a Roman and that Tully is an orator (for someone who does not know that Cicero and Tully are the same) will not be.

But we may now ask: in virtue of what will information be stored in the same location or in a different location? After all, there is nothing intrinsic to the idea of co-location which requires that co-located items should be related in any particular way. And surely the answer to the question is that the location will be the same when the information represents its object as the same. Thus mental files should be seen as a device for keeping track of when objects are coordinated (represented as-the-same) and, rather than understand coordination in terms of mental files, we should understand the workings of mental files in terms of coordination.

There are two other suggestions the referentialist might make to avoid having to adopt a relationist view. Suppose that I have two thoughts about an object. Then according to the first of these suggestions, what it is for me to represent the object as the same in these two thoughts is for me to have the additional thought that the objects *are* the same. Thus what it is to think that the individual Cicero is a Roman and then to have the coordinated thought that he is an orator is to think the additional thought that the one individual is the same as the other. But if the new thought is to have the desired effect, then it must be supposed that the individuals in the new thought are represented as the same as the respective individuals in the original thoughts; and so the account is circular. Indeed, strictly speaking, the account is not even correct (questions of circularity aside). For suppose I were to have two thoughts that I would express in the words "Cicero is a Roman" and "Tully is an orator." If I were then to have a thought that I would express in the words "Cicero = Tully," then this still would not guarantee that there was coordination within the original thoughts.

Just as with the semantical case (chapter 2, section B), we should be careful not to confuse representing two objects as the same with representing them as *being* the same, i.e. with having the thought that they are the same. As is evident from the semantic case, these two relationships are largely incompatible with one another, for I can only significantly represent two individuals as *being* the same if I do not already represent them *as* the same.

Confusion over this distinction often arises in discussion of mental files. It is often supposed, for example, that when I learn that Cicero is Tully, the two mental files associated with "Cicero" and "Tully" merge into a single mental file. But there is a double error here. I take it that the view must be that, in representing the individuals as *being* the same, I thereby represent them *as* the same since, otherwise, there is no reason to think that a merger would automatically take place. But this is not so. I can still recognize that I have learned something significant, viz. that Cicero is Tully, after being told that Cicero is Tully – which would not be so if I now represented the individuals as the same. Second, talk of merger is out of place. It is not that the merged file represents the individual as the same as the earlier files, since that would require that the earlier files represent the individual as the same. Rather, the new file, *if* I choose to create it, will represent the individual as *being* the same as the earlier files. Thus what happens, in effect, is that I *copy* the contents of the earlier files to a *new* file and perhaps even throw away the earlier files. But what we then have is supplementation or replacement rather than merger.

The other suggestion for dealing with coordination is not to add further content to the thoughts to be coordinated but to revise one's view of their underlying content. Thus to have the uncoordinated thought of Cicero's identity to Cicero (something one might express in the words "Cicero = Tully") is simply to have the thought that Cicero is identical to Cicero while to have the coordinated thought of Cicero's identity to Cicero (something one might express in the words "Cicero = Cicero") is to have the thought that Cicero is self-identical; and similarly for other cases of this sort (cf. Salmon, 1992).

The suggestion is intrinsically implausible. Surely "Cicero = Cicero" and "Cicero = Tully" are both dyadic predications, involving a single dyadic predicate "=" and two terms. It is highly unnatural to suppose that the use of the same name has the effect of converting what would otherwise be a dyadic predicate into the corresponding reflexive predicate or to suppose that there is only one reference to Cicero in the first sentence and yet two references to Cicero in the second. And what goes for the sentences also plausibly goes for the thoughts that we might express by their means.

The view amounts, in effect, to a refusal to admit the phenomenon of coordination. For coordination is most naturally understood as a way in which different references to or representations of a given object may be related. But the view would have us believe that what

appears to be a relationship between different references or representations is in reality a single occurrence. The thread that appears to
run through discourse or thought is bundled up into a ball!

In addition to its intrinsic implausibility, the view faces problems
over the possibility of coordination *across* thoughts rather than from
within a thought. Suppose that I judge that Cicero is a Roman and
then make the coordinated judgment that Cicero is an orator. Then,
at a stretch, I might regard this as a compound judgment to the effect
that Cicero is a Roman orator. But suppose now that I first *wonder*
whether Cicero is an orator and then make the coordinated judgment
that he is an orator. The current view requires us to take this to be
a single "thought" directed at a single content. But what is the
thought and what is the content? There is nothing sensible to
be said.

There are also some difficulties, of a more technical nature, over
accounting for coordination *within* a single thought. Consider a sentence, such as "Cicero loves Tully but Tully does not love Cicero,"
in which there are two coordinative links. Then what is the content
of a thought that we might express by its means? Do we first "reflexivize" with respect to "Cicero" and then with respect to "Tully,"
thereby getting the proposition that Cicero has the property of non-
reciprocally admiring Tully ($\lambda x(\lambda y(xAy \ \& \ {\sim}yAx)t)c$)? Or do we first
reflexivize with respect to "Tully" and then with respect to "Cicero,"
thereby getting the proposition that Tully has the property of being
non-reciprocally loved by Cicero ($\lambda y(\lambda x(xAy \ \& \ {\sim}yAx)c)t$)? Or do we
simultaneously reflexivize on "Cicero" and "Tully" (in that order),
thereby getting the proposition that Cicero stands in the relation of
non-reciprocally admiring Tully ($\lambda xy(xAy \ \& \ {\sim}yAx)ct$)? Or do we
simultaneously reflexivize in the opposite order thereby getting the
proposition that Tully stands in the relation of being non-reciprocally
loved by Cicero ($\lambda yx(xAy \ \& \ {\text{-}}yAx)tc$)? These propositions are all
clearly distinct (at least if the original distinctions upon which the
view depends can be made out). Yet there seems to be no basis for
preferring one reading of the sentence to another; and nor is it credible that the sentence or thought has no determinate content and is
ambiguous, so to speak, between the various different readings.[1]

We have yet to consider the most common intrinsicalist account
of intentional coordination; and this is the Fregean account in terms
of sense or modes of presentation. When an individual is represented

as the same in thought, according to this view, it is because the individual is presented in the same way; coordination is achieved through coincidence in "mode of presentation." Thus if I think that Cicero is a Roman and go on to think, in coordinated fashion, that he is an orator, then I must be thinking of Cicero under an identical mode of presentation – such as the ancient author of "On Friendship."

The major difficulty with this view, as in the semantical case, is to say in particular cases what the mode of presentation might be. As before, we may drive the point home by using a Bruce-type example (chapter 2, section A). We imagine that the inhabitant of a symmetric universe sees Bruce in "double" and, taking him to be two people, starts to have simultaneous thoughts with identical content about what each of the supposed two people is like (*he is wearing pink pajamas, he is smiling in a funny way*, etc.). It is clear that she is having *two* sets of singular thoughts about Bruce. It is also clear that the thoughts in each set are coordinated with one another but not with the thoughts of the other set. The Fregean must, therefore, suppose that Bruce is given through one mode of presentation in the one set of thoughts and through another mode of presentation in the other set of thoughts. But there is nothing sensible we can say as to what these modes of presentation might be. There can be no purely descriptive difference between them, since there is no purely descriptive difference in the way that our thinker conceives of the two Bruces; and there is no plausible non-descriptive difference in the two modes of presentation. If, for example, we take the difference to lie in the original sightings of Bruce, we then implausibly relate the content of the thoughts to the sightings and also appear to make it impossible for the thinker to continue to have coordinated thoughts about Bruce once she has lost all memory of the sightings.

This is, of course, a highly artificial example. In any actual case there are likely to be significant differences in what I believe about what I take to be two objects (even when they are in fact the same). But even in these cases it would often be a mistake to suppose that there was a difference in mode of presentation. Clearly, not every thought coordinate with a given singular belief will have some content that bears upon the mode of presentation of its object. There has to be a distinction between those thoughts whose content are somehow definitive of what the object is, or of how it is to be conceived, and those that are not. Now perhaps in cases of demonstrative reference and the like, there are certain thoughts that stand out as definitive of the object. But in most cases, there are no thoughts – or, at least, no individuating thoughts – that stand out in this way and that tell me, so to speak, what object my belief is about.

B.   Strict Co-representation

We therefore see that, just as in the case of language (chapter 2, section B), there is no plausible intrinsicalist account of coordination in thought. The various attempts to provide such an account – posed in terms of mental files, additional content, reconfigured form, or modes of presentation – all founder on one difficulty or another. What I would like to suggest in their place is a relational account along the lines of the previous semantic account: for a thought or thoughts to represent an object as the same is for it to be a representational requirement that the object of the thought or thoughts is the same. Thus just as the meaning of a language is given by a body of semantical requirements, which specify how the language means what it does, the intentionality of thought will be given by a body of representational requirements, which indicate how our various thoughts represent what they do; and coordination will be achieved in either case when those requirements demand an identity in what the language or thought is about.

We should distinguish, as before, between "pure" and "impure" requirements. Suppose that someone is thinking about Cicero, but not as the famous Roman orator. Then there is a sense in which his thought is of the famous Roman orator. But this is not a pure representational requirement on the thought. Rather it is something that follows from the pure representational fact that he is thinking of Cicero and the non-representational fact that Cicero is the famous Roman orator.

We should also distinguish, as before, between the representational facts and the representational requirements. Suppose that I have the thoughts that Cicero is a Roman and that Tully is an orator (without knowing that Cicero is Tully). It is then a representational fact that the first thought is of Cicero and a representational fact that the second thought is of Cicero and hence a representational fact that both thoughts are of the same object. But it is not a representational *requirement* that both thoughts be of the same object. The representational requirements constitute a body of information accessible in principle to the thinker and need only be closed under manifest, as opposed to classical, consequence.

There are some features of intentional representation that are worthy of special note. Suppose a sentence signifies a proposition containing two occurrences of a given object, say the proposition that Cicero is the same as Cicero. There will then presumably be two constituent expressions of the sentence (an occurrence of "Cicero" and an occurrence of "Tully," say), each responsible for putting its own occurrence of the object into the proposition. But suppose now that a thought signifies a proposition containing two occurrences of a given object, say the proposition that this man is the same as that man (it is better for the purposes of the example if the thought is not expressed in words, but is a "felt" identity). Then it is not clear that there must be two components of the thought, each responsible for putting its occurrence of the object into the proposition. Thoughts do not appear to have the same kind of clear syntax as sentences.

This then creates a difficulty if we want to talk of coordination within a thought. For between what do we coordinate? What I would like to suggest is that it may still be correct to talk of a thought being of an object in a given occurrence or position in such cases, even though there may be no corresponding constituent of the thought. Thus in the example of the felt identity above, we may distinguish between the first and the second object of the thought (even when the objects are the same) and hence we may sensibly say that it is, or is not, representationally required that the "first" object be the same as the "second" object of the thought. This provides, by the way, yet another reason not to think of coordination syntactically in terms of the repeated use of the same symbol. For in the intentional cases, it may be hard to say what the symbol or symbol-surrogate should be taken to be.

Another significant difference between semantic and intentional representation is that semantic requirements are for the most part "up to us" while representational requirements are not. We are free to adopt different conventions governing the meaning of our terms but we are not generally free to adopt different rules governing the content of our thoughts – of our memories and perceptions, for example – except in so far as the content is itself conveyed by means of language of a conventional sort. For this reason, talk of representational *requirements* may be misleading since it may appear to suggest that *we* impose the requirements on thought. If anything, the representational character of thought is something that imposes itself upon us rather than being something that we impose on it. But, of course, these various differences do not stand in the way of providing a relational treatment of thought that is, by and large, analogous to our relational treatment of language.

C.   The Content of Thought

I believe that the relational view enables the referentialist to provide a much more plausible account of the content of thought. Perhaps the best way to bring this out is by considering a purely intentional version of Frege's puzzle, one that makes no reference to language. It is this puzzle, or something like it, that has led many philosophers to endorse senses or "modes of presentation" at the level of thought, even if not at the level of language; and so it is worth showing how this unpalatable conclusion may be avoided.

Essential to the formulation of the puzzle will be such locutions at "the belief that Cicero is an orator"; and it is important to be clear on how they are being used. First, I have in mind *token* beliefs. Your beliefs, in this sense, will never be the same as mine. Second, there is a sense of belief – and especially for the referentialist – in which someone's belief that Cicero is an orator is the same as his belief that Tully is an orator and in which to have the one belief is to have the other belief. But there is also a sense – much more natural to my mind – in which these beliefs are not the same and in which to have the one belief is not necessarily to have the other. A reflective person who had the belief that Cicero is an orator in this other sense would be willing to express his belief in the words "Cicero is an orator," even though he would not be willing to express it in the words "Tully is an orator"; and similarly for the belief that Tully is an orator.

It seems clear, with this understanding of the locution, that someone's belief (at a given time) that Cicero is an orator might not be the same as his belief (at that time) that Tully is an orator. We therefore have the first assumption of the puzzle:

1   *Doxastic Difference*: The belief that Cicero is an orator is not the same as the belief that Tully is an orator.

We also assume:

2   *Doxastic Link*: If the beliefs are different, then their contents are different.

I take "content" here in the broadest sense to include not only what is believed but also the representational manner in which it is believed (should there be such a thing). Thus if Peter represents Paderewski as a famous Polish pianist in believing that Paderewski is musical then it will be part of the content of his belief that Paderewski is so represented. Doxastic Link is then very plausible. Weird split-mind cases aside, how could someone have two distinct beliefs whose contents in this broad sense were the same? How could they simultaneously believe the same thing twice unless they represented what they believed in different ways?

We must now say something about the content of the beliefs. It is plausible to suppose that the content of the belief that Cicero is an orator has an objectual component corresponding to the use of the name "Cicero" in the ascription of the belief and a predicative component corresponding to the use of the predicate phrase "is an orator" and that the content of the belief is the result of "predicatively putting together" the objectual component and the predicative component (and similarly for the belief that Tully is an orator). It, therefore, follows that:

3   *Compositionality*: If the contents of the beliefs are different, then so are the objectual components.

We might take the *object of* a belief to be what it is about. Thus the object of the belief that Cicero is an orator is Cicero. One might then think that there can be no more to the objectual component of a belief than what it is about.

4   *Objectual Link*: If the objectual components are different than so are the objects.

But evidently:

5   *Objectual Identity*: The objects of the two beliefs are the same.

We now have a contradiction and so at least one of the assumptions should be given up.

The linguistic and non-linguistic versions of the puzzle are roughly analogous (with beliefs and subject-components in the non-linguistic version taking the place of sentences and names in the linguistic version). However, referentialists (though not Fregeans) have tended to adopt very different lines of response to the two versions of the puzzle. In the case of the linguistic version, they have denied Cognitive Difference or Cognitive Link; they have, therefore, thought that, despite appearances, there is no semantic or relevant cognitive difference between the sentences "Cicero is an orator" and "Tully is an orator." However, in the case of the non-linguistic version, it has not seemed plausible to deny the corresponding assumptions of Doxastic Difference or Doxastic Link. Some other assumption must, therefore, be rejected; and the only plausible candidate to present itself is Objectual Link. It must be allowed, in other words, that the objectual components of the two beliefs are not the same even though the objects are.

This immediately raises the question of what the objectual component might be and, again, the only plausible view is that it is something akin to a Fregean sense or manner of presentation. Thus the content of the belief on this view will include, or involve, a mode of presentation by which its object is given. This could in principle be given by the name by means of which the belief is naturally described – thus the mode of presentation of Cicero in the belief that Cicero is an orator might be something like *the referent of* "Cicero"; but it is more plausibly taken to be something non-linguistic.

Many referentialists have felt obliged, for reasons of this sort, to adopt a differential position on the content of thought and language; intentional reference is mediated through – or inextricably associated with – sense or modes of presentation, while linguistic reference is not. But such a position (we might call it "back-door Fregeanism") is quite bizarre. I may express a belief of mine in the words "Cicero is an orator." The simplest and most natural view is that there is no more to the content of my belief than there is to the content of my words; I say what I believe. Indeed, if this were not so, then there would appear to be a serious failure in communication; the attempt – or, at least, the most natural attempt – to express my belief would always fall short of the full content of what I believe.

It is also odd to suppose that there should be any fundamental difference in the general representational character of language and thought. For one thing, it is not at all clear to what extent there *are* two systems of representation. The simple-minded among us may perhaps be forgiven for thinking that the English speaker by and large thinks in English and the French speaker in French. But nor is it clear, even if the systems of representation are by and large disjoint, why they should differ in this way. For how can the *vehicle* of representation – be it speech or writing or thought – make any difference to its representational character? And why, in particular, should thought lose its wonderful colors once it is translated into the garb of ordinary language?

These difficulties disappear once we adopt the relational point of view. For on this view, the content of a belief will be given by a coordinated rather than by an uncoordinated proposition. Thus we may distinguish between the content of the belief that Cicero is Tully (where this is the negatively coordinated proposition) from the content of the belief that Cicero is Cicero (where this is the positively coordinated proposition). This is already a great advance on the usual referentialist view, which is unable to make any such distinction without either distorting the logical form or appealing to some notion of sense or "guise."

More significantly still, we should now distinguish between the collective and the individual content of someone's beliefs. If asked what someone believes, then it would normally be thought sufficient to respond by listing the various propositions that he believes. But this view can no longer be sustained. For suppose that someone believes that Cicero is a Roman and also believes that Cicero is an orator. Then what he believes is the proposition that Cicero is a Roman and the proposition that Cicero is an orator. But suppose now that he believes that Cicero is a Roman and also believes that Tully is an orator. Then the individual content of his two beliefs is as before: the proposition that Cicero is a Roman; and the proposition that Tully (i.e. Cicero) is an orator. But there is a difference in the coordinated content of the two beliefs; for, in the one case, the beliefs are positively coordinated while, in the other case, they are not. Thus the coordinated content of his beliefs, taken collectively, is not exhausted, or even determined, by the content of his beliefs, taken individually.[2] We might think of there being coordinative threads running from one belief or thought to another. Once we cut through the threads and consider the beliefs or thoughts on their own, there is no knowing from their individual contents how they are to be reassembled.

Applying these considerations to the puzzle, we see how two beliefs might be different even though their intrinsic content is the same (in violation of Doxastic Link). If someone were properly to reduplicate a belief, he would have to form a belief whose intrinsic content was the same and which, *in addition*, was appropriately coordinated with the content of the original belief. But this is not what happens when someone believes that Cicero is an orator and then forms the belief that Tully is an orator. For in this case, the content of the subsequent belief is not appropriately coordinated with the content of the original belief, even though the content of the two beliefs is the same. Thus if one takes into account the content of someone's beliefs as a whole, then there will be a difference between believing the same content "twice," though in uncoordinated fashion, and believing it "once"; and it is only if one neglects the collective aspect of content that one will be tempted into thinking that the case is impossible and that there must be some intrinsic difference in the content of the two beliefs.

If the discussion of this case is on the right lines, then it should be possible to adopt a strictly referential position while still holding on to the representational uniformity of language and thought. We have previously noted a couple of ways in which relationism is capable of rescuing the standard form of referentialism from some of its less desirable consequences. It can respect the intuitive difference in meaning between "Cicero is Cicero" and "Cicero is Tully"; and it can accommodate our access to the semantic facts. We now have another major respect in which this is so; for we see that referentialism no longer requires us to posit a fundamental disparity in the representational mechanisms of language and of thought.

D.   The Cognitive Puzzle

We come at last to the cognitive version of Frege's puzzle. There is a clear cognitive difference between the sentences "Cicero is an orator" and "Tully is an orator" – one can learn something different upon being told one as opposed to the other. But how, on a relational view, can we account for this cognitive difference without appealing to an intrinsic difference in their semantic content?

In discussing this question, it will be helpful to spell out the notion of cognitive difference with a bit more precision than is usual. To this end, let us imagine a communication between two people who possess a common language. One of them asserts a certain sentence in that language – say "Cicero is an orator" – and thereby conveys some information to the other. Prior to the communication, the hearer will possess certain information, which we may call the *cognitive base*. Let us call the asserted sentence the *input* and the enlarged body of information that the hearer possesses as a result of the communication the *cognitive impact*. Thus relative to a cognitive base I, an input s will have a certain cognitive impact J (something which we might symbolize as: $I \oplus s = J$).

We should distinguish between cognitive impact and cognitive potential. The cognitive *potential of* a sentence is the function that takes each cognitive base into the cognitive impact of the sentence on the base (in other words, for given s, it is the function $\lambda I(I \oplus s)$). Thus the *cognitive potential* of a sentence will tell us what cognitive impact the sentence will have on any given cognitive base. Cognitive impact and cognitive potential are two things that might reasonably be meant by "cognitive significance." However, a full solution to Frege's puzzle should provide us with a general explanation of a sentence's cognitive potential, i.e. of the cognitive impact it would have upon any given base.

There are two somewhat different ways in which one might attempt to account for the cognitive potential of a sentence, one lying at the level of "thought" or "content" and the other at the level of "language." On the one hand, we may focus on the non-linguistic information that the hearer acquires, rather than on the linguistic means by which it is acquired. Our task is then to provide an account of what that information is, given the sentence asserted by the speaker and the non-linguistic information already known to the hearer. On the other hand, we may focus, not merely on the non-linguistic information that the hearer acquires, but also on the linguistic means by which it is acquired. Our task is then to explain how, through their understanding of a common language, the speaker is able to convey the information that he does to the hearer.

The Fregean succeeds admirably at both tasks. On his view, the sentence "Cicero is an orator" expresses a certain thought or proposition; and this is the non-linguistic information that the hearer acquires from the speaker. *How* he acquires this information is schematically as follows. Given the speaker's assertion of "Cicero is an orator," the hearer knows that the sentence is true; and given his understanding of the language, the speaker knows that if the sentence is true then Cicero is an orator. He is thereby able to infer that Cicero is an orator.

It might appear as if the referentialist can do equally well, since nothing in the above account would seem to depend upon adopting a Fregean view of content. Thus the content of "Cicero is an orator" would now be a singular proposition rather than a Fregean thought. It is this that gets added to the hearer's information; and the way it gets added is through the hearer knowing what is required for the sentence to be true. The only difference in the two positions would appear to lie in what they think belongs where. For the referentialist will take the cognitive difference between "Cicero is an orator" and "Tully is an orator" to belong "upstairs," at the level of language, and not also "downstairs," at the level of thought.

We have had reason to reject the Fregean response, since it postulates an untenable distinction of sense, but it seems to me that the standard referentialist response is also untenable. The appearance of adequacy arises from focusing on the special case in which the cognitive base is "empty," or devoid of relevant information. But suppose that the hearer already has some information that he would express in the words "Cicero is Roman" though not any information that he would express in the words "Tully is Roman," notwithstanding his being competent in the use of both names. Then on being told "Cicero is an orator," he would learn the singular proposition that Cicero is a Roman orator and thereby be able to infer that there is a Roman orator. But this is not something he could do upon being told "Tully is an orator," since he would not be in a position to "put together" the information conveyed with the information he already has. Thus he obtains some non-linguistic information in the one case that he does not obtain in the other even though the non-linguistic information conveyed by the two input sentences is the same.

The reasons why this is a *special* problem for the referentialist is that he must work with a conception of propositional knowledge that is closed under manifest rather than classical consequence. Given that a thinker knows the proposition that x Fs and also knows the proposition that x Gs, he does not necessarily know the proposition that x both Fs and Gs, no matter how logically competent he may be. The referentialist, therefore, faces the problem of explaining how the propositions can be "put together" through the use of "Cicero" though not through the use of "Tully." The Fregean, on the other hand, can work with the classical notion of consequence since it will be apparent to the hearer when the sense by which the object is given in the two premises is the same.

In the face of this difficulty, most referentialists would be tempted to go linguistic.[3] It would be supposed, in the first case, that the hearer knows the truth of the *sentences* "Cicero is Roman" and "Cicero is an orator." From these, he infers the truth of the sentence "Cicero is a Roman orator"; and from this, he then infers, given his understanding of the language, that Cicero is a Roman orator. Thus he makes the required inference at the level of language and it is only once he has made the inference at this level that he descends to the level of thought. In the second case, by contrast, the corresponding inference at the level of language cannot be made and so the speaker has no means of acquiring the relevant non-linguistic information.

In going linguistic, the referentialists have implicitly abandoned the possibility of providing an account of the inferential process at the level of thought. This is highly suspect in itself. For the inference will present itself to the hearer as going from the premises that Cicero is Roman and that Cicero is an orator to the conclusion that Cicero is a Roman orator; it will not represent itself as an inference that makes a detour through the language by which these propositions are expressed. And, in general, there is something quite bizarre about the idea that, in drawing out the logical consequences of a given set of propositions, it should be necessary to reason explicitly about the language by which the propositions are expressed.

To make matters worse, the linguistic account does not even work on its own terms. The problem is with the inference from the truth of "Cicero is Roman" and the truth of "Cicero is an orator" to the truth of "Cicero is a Roman orator." For whether the hearer is justified in making this inference will depend upon his having the same "take" on the name "Cicero" in the two premises. If, for example, he thinks there are two uses of the name "Cicero," one for the statesman and the other for the orator – just as in Kripke's "Paderewski" example – then the inference will be no more justified than the corresponding inference from the truth of "Cicero is Roman" and "Tully is an orator."

Thus the referentialist account faces the same problem at the level of the names as it faced at the level of the objects. Just as the inference from the two propositions concerning the individual Cicero is not necessarily warranted, neither is the inference from the two propositions concerning the name "Cicero." Of course, we know in both cases that the inference *is* justified but the problem is to provide some explanation, compatible with the referentialist semantics, as to why this should be so. In going linguistic, the inferential phenomenon which the referentialist was trying to explain at the level of objects has simply been reduplicated at the level of language.

Indeed, we can generalize the previous difficulties to obtain a sweeping objection to any other account of cognitive potential that the standard referentialist might provide. Given that we are in possession of the information that a Fs and the information that a Gs, it appears that we are sometimes justified in putting this information "together" and inferring that a both Fs and Gs. But how? The natural hypothesis – and the only one to which it would appear that the standard referentialist can appeal – is that we are in possession of some further information I and that this information, along with the given premises, justifies us in inferring the desired conclusion. Now presumably, this further information will also justify us in "putting together" the information from the two premises when the properties F and G in question are strengthened in a purely qualitative way. Thus the further information will justify us in inferring the conclusion that x has the property F & P & G & Q from the premises that x has the property F & P and x has the property G & Q, no matter what the purely qualitative properties P and Q might be. But it can now be demonstrated that in these circumstances the thinker must be in possession of a complete purely qualitative description of x. In other words, there must be some purely qualitative property R which is such that he is justified in inferring from what he already knows that x has R and is qualitatively indiscernible from any other object that has R.[4]

Thus adjunctive inference from singular propositions becomes impossible without qualitative individuation of the objects involved.

This comes close to constituting a reductio of the referentialist's position. For they have usually supposed that a speaker may have the use of a name without possessing the means by which its bearer might be distinguished from other objects that are qualitatively distinguishable from it. But what the above argument shows is that if this were so, then the name could not play its normal role in inference and communication. Thus it appears that the cognitive version of Frege's puzzle requires the referentialist to posit something akin to Fregean sense after all, though not for the usual reasons.

These difficulties in the referentialist position disappear, once again, upon adopting a relationist view. We wish to explain how the hearer might be justified in inferring that Cicero is a Roman orator when he already knows that Cicero is Roman and is told "Cicero is an orator," though not when he is told "Tully is an orator." For the relationist, the singular proposition that Cicero is a Roman will be added to the hearer's informational base in either case. However, there is a crucial difference. For in the first case, the proposition is not merely added to the base but appropriately coordinated with the propositions in it – and, in particular, with the proposition that Cicero is Roman. But in the second case, the proposition is not coordinated with the other propositions in the base – or, at least, not in the same way. It is then evident that the inference to Cicero being a Roman orator will be justified in the first case, when the premises are coordinated, though not in the second case, when the premises remain uncoordinated.[5]

We see that the *relative* difference in meaning between the names is sufficient to account for the difference in cognitive significance, for it is essentially in terms of the relative difference that we account for whether or not the new information will coordinate with the pre-existing information. Nor is there any difficulty, as there was for the standard referentialist, in seeing the inference as being justified at the level of content, rather than by means of a linguistic detour. Indeed, the reasoning from the inside will look just the same as it does under the Fregean approach. But where the Fregean sees sameness of sense, the relationist finds only coordination in content.

There is, however, a fundamental respect in which the relationist approach is quite different from the Fregean approach *and* the standard referentialist alternative. For the Fregeans and the standard referentialists both adopt a simple incremental model of information transmission; to learn something – to acquire new information – is simply to add it to what is already known (along perhaps with the consequences of the resulting knowledge). But this simple incremental model must now be dropped in favour of an interactive model. For the new information that we acquire may or may not coordinate with what is already known; and how it coordinates, or "engages," with what we already know will make a difference to what we subsequently come to learn. We do not merely add something to the pot; we also give it a stir.

This difference in approach results in a curious compromise between the two other views. For the standard referentialist, the information associated with a name is irrelevant to its cognitive significance, i.e. to the contribution it makes to the cognitive impact of the sentences that contain it. For the Fregean, by contrast, some of the information associated with the name will be constitutive of its meaning; and this will be relevant to its cognitive significance, even though the rest is not. The relationist agrees with the Fregean on the relevance of the associated information, but he disagrees both on *how* it is relevant and on the *extent* to which it is relevant. For it will not be relevant through constituting the meaning of the name and hence being part of what is conveyed by the sentential input. Rather, it will be relevant through being constitutive of what one already knows and hence a determinant, along with the sentential input, of cognitive impact. This difference is dramatically illustrated in the case of the empty cognitive base. Suppose that the hearer originally knows nothing about the bearers of "Cicero" and "Tully." Then on the relationist view, he gains no substantive non-linguistic information upon being told "Cicero = Tully" while, on the Fregean view, he learns what we would learn in any other case, viz. that the senses associated with the names are of the same object. Furthermore, the *whole* of the information associated with the name will be relevant for the relationist in this special way; for the whole of it will be capable, without distinction, of engaging with what else he learns.

Even for those cases in which we do associate some identifying information with a name, the Fregean view would appear to be based upon an untenable distinction between that information which is constitutive of the meaning of the name and that which is not. One does not need to be a Quinean sceptic about the analytic/synthetic distinction to believe that the distinction has no clear application in the case of names. Of everything that I know concerning the bearer of a name, there is nothing – or, at least, very little – that stands out as constitutive of its meaning. It is a great advantage of the relational approach that it can give due recognition to the cognitive significance of the information we associate with a name – and thereby do justice to a key Fregean insight – without having to maintain that any of that information is of a peculiarly semantical sort.

Chapter 4

Coordination between Speakers

We have seen that there can be coordination within language and within thought. But there are two other directions in which it may obtain. In the first place, there can be coordination between language and thought (as was implicit in the discussion of Frege's cognitive puzzle). Thus suppose I express a belief in the words "Cicero is an orator." Then it is natural to suppose that the object of my belief is coordinated with the subject of my sentence; it is a semantico-intentional requirement that they be the same. Or again, suppose I use the term "this" to refer to an object that I am currently perceiving. Then it is natural to suppose that the object of my perception, or of my state of attending to the object, is coordinated with the referent of the term.

In the second place, and perhaps more significantly, there can be coordination from speaker to speaker (or, more generally, from speaker or thinker to speaker or thinker). Perhaps a paradigm case is when I derive my use of a name from someone else. Our two uses of the name are then naturally taken to be coordinated. But there are many other cases of cross-speaker coordination. Suppose, for example, that an object is in common view and that we communicate about it by means of the pronoun "it." The various uses of the pronoun are then coordinated; they represent the object as the same and someone who did not know that they were being used to refer to the *same* object, even if he knew that each of them referred to the object, would have failed to understand what was being said.

These cases of language-to-thought and speaker-to-speaker coordination raise many interesting questions and clearly are of great significance in understanding how thoughts are conveyed from one speaker to another. But in what follows I should like to focus on some puzzles, first pointed out by Kripke (1979), that arise from our attempt to report what others believe. These are essentially puzzles concerning the coordination of the language of the reporter with the thought of the believer. But since the believer may verbalize his thought, it is also possible to regard them as puzzles concerning the coordination of the language of the reporter with the language of the believer. I should like to argue that these puzzles raise very real difficulties and that is only by going relational that they can be solved.

I begin with an exposition of the puzzle, designed to meet certain obvious objections and to bring out what is genuinely at issue (section A). I go on to consider some related puzzles, which show that the original puzzle has nothing essentially to do either with names or with belief (section B). I then offer a relational solution to these puzzles – first at a relatively superficial pre-semantic level (sections C and D), next at a deeper semantic level (sections E and F) and, finally, when only variables – not names – are involved (section G). The final solution brings together the previous relational treatment of variables with the present approach to belief reports. Our treatment of the puzzle constitutes a strong argument in favor of referentialism since, given the radical form of relationism to which we must appeal, it is hard to see how it might be replicated at the level of sense (section H).

A.   Kripke's Puzzle

Kripke states two main versions of the puzzle – one concerning the bilingual Pierre and his beliefs about London and the other concerning the monolingual Peter and his beliefs about Paderewski. I shall focus on the second version since it brings into sharper relief the issues I wish to discuss, but my remarks will apply, mutatis mutandis, to the first version.

The puzzle goes as follows. Peter overhears some conversations concerning the great Polish pianist and statesman, Paderewski, and comes to the view that they concern two individuals, one a pianist and the other a statesman. Since he believes that all pianists are musical, he has a belief which he would express in the words "Paderewski is musical"; and it would therefore appear to be true to say that Peter believes that Paderewski is musical.[1] Since Peter believes that all statesman are not musical, he has a belief which he would express in the words "Paderewski is not musical"; and it would, therefore, appear to be true to say that Peter believes that Paderewski is not musical. But surely Peter does not both believe that Paderewski is musical and that Paderewski is not musical. Indeed, Peter may be the leading logician of the land, who would never let an explicit contradiction escape his attention.

The reasoning of the puzzle can be seen to rest on two implicit assumptions. The first, Disquotation, is meant to justify the transition from Peter's assenting to the sentence "Paderewski is (not) musical" to our reporting him as believing that Paderewski is (not) musical. The second, Consistency, is meant to rule out the possibility that a rational person, such as Peter, might believe both that S and that not S.

I believe that the puzzle is much more difficult and far-reaching than is commonly supposed; and so before considering our own solution to the puzzle, I would like to consider various ways in which the presentation of the puzzle might be modified or extended. The modifications will serve to ward off certain common lines of attack, while the extensions will show that the puzzle has nothing essential to do with our use of names or even with our practice of reporting beliefs and other propositional attitudes.

Let me begin by discussing a number of ways in which the presentation might be modified or improved.

Assent

It is not altogether clear how to formulate the Disquotation Principle. For the purposes of the puzzle, its application can be restricted to non-indexical sentences that are used unambiguously. However, even in this case, mere assent is not enough to guarantee belief, since it may not be sincere or given reflectively. Perhaps sincere and reflective assent by a normal speaker of the language *is* enough to guarantee belief (Kripke, 1979, pp. 112–13). But it is perhaps preferable to avoid such difficulties by formulating Disquotation in terms of *expression* rather than *assent*. For there is an ordinary intuitive notion of someone's expressing what he believes; and, given that someone does indeed give expression to what he believes, there is then no question but that the conditions of his assent are of a kind to which it is intended that the Disquotation Principle should apply.

Truth versus correctness

Kripke formulates his puzzles in terms of the *truth* of various belief reports. But many philosophers have wanted to distinguish the *truth* of a report, which is a purely semantic matter, from its *correctness*, which may be a partly pragmatic matter. Thus they have wanted to maintain that it may be true to say "Peter believes that Paderewski is musical" and true to say "Peter believes that Paderewski is not musical" and yet, because of various pragmatic factors, it may be incorrect or misleading to say both of these things. Thus the puzzle is solved once we realize that our disinclination to take both reports to be true arises from our failure to distinguish the question of their truth from the question of their correctness.

There is no need to engage with these philosophers on the alleged distinction between truth and correctness, for we can pose the puzzle exclusively in terms of the *correctness* of the various belief-reports, rather than their *truth*, and leave on one side the question of whether or how they might diverge. Thus what we must now maintain, in stating the puzzle, is that it is correct to report Peter as believing that Paderewski is musical and also correct to report Peter as believing that Paderewski is not musical and yet not correct to report him as believing both. Any solution that depends upon distinguishing between the truth and the correctness of a belief report will then be irrelevant to the puzzle, as it still remains unclear how the individual belief reports can be correct even though the composite belief report is not.

Context

Another common response to the puzzle is to suppose that, in making the individual belief reports, we are implicitly appealing to different contexts for the use of the name, one corresponding to Peter's conception of him as a pianist and the other to Peter's conception of him as a statesman. Thus it is as if we had said "Peter believes that Paderewski the pianist is musical" and "Peter believes that Paderewski the statesman is not musical." There would then be no difficulty in seeing why each individual report should be regarded as correct. And nor would there be any difficulty in accounting for our disinclination to regard the composite report as correct since we would naturally understand it as appealing to a single context for the use of the name. Thus the puzzle would again rest on an equivocation, not now in the standards of assessment (truth versus correctness) but in the context of use ("Paderewski the pianist" versus "Paderewski the statesman").

It is perhaps unfortunate that, in presenting the puzzle, Kripke first describes Peter's situation to the reader and then asks him, the reader, to determine what belief reports he should make in the light of what he knows, since this way of presenting the puzzle leads to the possibility of there being a "mental" shift in the context of use. But let us imagine instead that we, who are in the know, are assessing the belief reports of someone else, say Sue, who is not in the know. We might suppose that she knows next to nothing about Peter. She perhaps knows that Peter has the use of the name "Paderewski," though not that it is "fractured"; and she perhaps knows that Peter has beliefs about Paderewski that he is only capable of expressing by means of the name "Paderewski." But she is totally in the dark, we may suppose, about any of Peter's specific beliefs.

She is now asked to make a guess about what Peter believes concerning Paderewski. Perhaps a range of possible answers are written down on some cards (the "report" cards) and she is asked to hold up those cards whose content she is prepared to endorse. If she were to hold up the card reporting that Peter believes that Paderewski is musical, we would judge her answer to be correct; and similarly if she were to hold up the card reporting that Peter believes that Paderewski is not musical. However, we would not judge her answer to be correct if she were to hold up both of these cards (and nor is she likely to think that such an answer could correctly report Peter's beliefs, given that he is rational).

Our assessments of correctness are the same as in the case in which the respondent is "in the know"; and yet there is no reason, in the present case, to suppose that the context in which the name was used could somehow shift in interpretation from "Paderewski the pianist" to "Paderewski the statesman." Indeed, there is no difficulty in supposing that the context of use (as given by the external circumstances and Sue's prior mental state) is exactly the same for each of the belief reports; and we have so described the case that the reports are not made one after the other but hypothetically at the very same time.

Thus there is not even the possibility of one of the individual reports creating a different context for the use of the other report.

Consistency

Implicit in the formulation of the puzzle is the assumption that we cannot correctly attribute a pair of contradictory beliefs to a rational person and this has led some philosophers to doubt whether this is indeed true under the intended understanding of the belief reports. However, the question of what a rational person might believe is not really at issue. After all, the leading logician of the land may be Graham Priest and, arguably, he is rational and could correctly be said to possess contradictory beliefs.

What is really at issue is a question of coordination. In reporting Peter's beliefs, my use of the name "Paderewski" is coordinated; I take myself to be making the very same use of the name "Paderewski" from one belief report to the other. However, Peter would not be willing to express his beliefs in a correspondingly coordinated fashion; he would not be willing to assert "Paderewski is musical" and "Paderewski is not musical" with what he took to be the same use of the name "Paderewski." The critical question, therefore, is whether the reporting of beliefs, in the intended sense, requires *co-coordination* between reporter and believer: if the reporter's use of various names is coordinated in the report of the beliefs, then should the corresponding use of the names be correspondingly coordinated in the believer's expression of his beliefs?

The case of contradictory beliefs raises this issue in a particular acute form, since it might then be thought to be impossible for a rational believer to coordinate the expression of his beliefs in the same manner as the reporter coordinates the report of those beliefs. But the same question also arises in cases in which the believer is able to make the coordination. Suppose, for example, that Peter draws no inferences from his beliefs about Paderewski. He believes that the one Paderewski is a pianist; he believes of what he takes to be the other Paderewski that he is a statesman; and that is it. We can then still raise the question of whether he should be reported as believing both that Paderewski is a pianist and that Paderewski is a statesman; and presumably our answer in this case will be the same as when the beliefs are contradictory.

De dicto belief

It is critical to establishing a genuine puzzle that it be shown that the various judgments of correctness should hold under an unequivocal reading of the belief reports. For it might be allowed that there is a reading of the individual belief reports in which it is correct to say that Peter believes that Paderewski is musical and also correct to say that Peter believes that Paderewski is not musical; and it might also be allowed that there is a reading of the composite belief report in which it is incorrect to say both that Peter believes that Paderewski is musical and that Peter believes that Paderewski is not musical; but it may be denied that there is a single reading under which the individual belief reports are correct and the composite belief report is incorrect.

Kripke attempts to secure an unequivocal reading by insisting that the belief reports should be understood as de dicto (pp. 105–6). What we are reporting is that Peter believes that: Paderewski is (or is not) musical. Thus the name must occur within the scope of the belief operator. I myself doubt that considerations of scope might serve to distinguish the reading that Kripke has in mind; and it is especially odd for a Millian to think that they might since names, on his view, are most plausibly taken to be "scopeless."

There is, however, another sense in which a belief report may be said to be de dicto. For it may be de dicto in the sense of aiming to be faithful to how the believer himself would express his beliefs; there should be an appropriate match, if the report is to be correct, between the embedded clause that the reporter uses in making his report and the sentence or "dictum" that the believer might use in expressing his belief. Of course, de dicto in this sense is somewhat vague, since it is not altogether clear what is meant by "fidelity" or "match." But it does seem plausible that the report that Peter believes that Paderewski is musical *is* faithful to how Peter might express his belief, as is the report that Peter believes that Paderewski is not musical. And it is also plausible that the report that Peter believes both that Paderewski is musical and that Paderewski is not musical is *not* faithful to how Peter would express his beliefs – for we use a pair of sentences we know to be contradictory in reporting his beliefs and yet Peter would not use a pair of sentences he knew to be contradictory in expressing his beliefs.

Composite reports

In posing the puzzle, Kripke tends to operate in the material mode (questions of assent aside). Thus he directly asks us to consider whether Peter does or does not believe that Paderewski is musical. We, on the other hand, have tended to operate in the formal mode. In discussing the puzzle, we have asked, not whether Peter believes such and such, but whether a given belief report is or is not correct. Of course, this is important if we want to keep the distinction between truth and correctness firmly in mind (if we merely *make* the reports then it may not be clear whether it is their truth or their correctness that is in question). But it is important for a more significant reason. For it enables us, at least in principle, to distinguish between the correctness of a composite report and the correctness of the individual reports that make it up. If we find ourselves making each of the two individual reports, then the question of whether we are willing to make both reports would hardly seem to arise. But if we focus our attention on the reports themselves, then it would appear possible to distinguish between the correctness of the reports, when considered in isolation from one another, and the correctness of the reports, when considered together.

On this way of thinking, Disquotation, or something like it, will guarantee the correctness of the individual belief reports while Consistency, or something like it, will guarantee the incorrectness of the composite report. But we must now make a further assumption before we get an outright contradiction. For we must assume that the composite belief report will be correct if the individual belief reports which make it up are correct. Although this might look like a distinction without a difference, we shall later argue that it is only by giving up this assumption that the puzzle can be solved.

External links

The basis for the application of Disquotation is that reporter and believer should share the common use of a name such as "Paderewski." But there is a special case of shared common use which makes the application of the principle extremely problematic. For suppose that Peter had a twin, Petrov, who likes to do everything that Peter does. Now Peter has two uses of the name "Paderewski," which we may dub "Paderewski [pianist]" and "Paderewski [statesman]"; and we may suppose that Petrov derives a use of the name from Peter's use of "Paderewski [pianist]" and another use from Peter's use of "Paderewski [statesman]." Thus Petrov's use of the name is fractured in exactly the same way as Peter's. Then, contrary to Disquotation, it is not clear that it would be correct for Petrov to report Peter as believing that Paderewski [pianist] is not musical or as believing that Paderewski [statesman] is musical. Indeed, I think we have a strong intuition that Petrov should report Peter as *not* believing that Paderewski [pianist] is not musical and as *not* believing that Paderewski [statesman] is musical.

We may avoid problematic applications of this sort, and actually make the application of the principle even stronger, by supposing that each of Peter's two uses of the name is directly derived from the reporter's use of the name. Thus we may suppose that Peter picks up his uses of the name from some conversations with the reporter and that the reporter then makes the same use of the name in reporting what Peter believes (perhaps even forgetting the content of the original conversations). In what follows we shall implicitly assume that all of the relevant cases are of this sort.

B.   Some Related Puzzles

I have considered various ways in which the presentation of Kripke's puzzle might be modified or improved. I would now like to consider some related puzzles. These make it even harder to see how the original puzzle is to be solved. For any solution to the original puzzle should solve – or, at least, be extendable to a solution of – these other puzzles. But it is often hard if not impossible to see how, in the case of particular solutions that have been proposed, this might be done.[2]

A one-premise version

Let us begin by presenting a compact one-premise version of the puzzle. This will be useful for expository purposes and will have certain dialectical advantages over the standard presentation.

The idea behind this formulation is that one may correctly report Peter as realizing that Paderewski is pianist but as not realizing both that Paderewski is a pianist and that Paderewski is a statesman.[3] For we may suppose that it is the intention of the speaker to report Peter as realizing that Paderewski is a pianist but as not having a coordinated belief that that very person is also a statesman. It then seems perfectly appropriate for the speaker to indicate the deficiency in Peter's beliefs in the way we have supposed ("Peter fails to realize both that Paderewski is a pianist and that Paderewski is a statesman"). This is not to deny that there might be a reading under which the report is not correct but there would also appear to be a reading – and perhaps the most natural one at that – under which it *is* correct.

But if it is correct to report Peter as realizing that Paderewski is a pianist but as not realizing both that Paderewski is a pianist and that Paderewski is a statesman then, by considerations of symmetry, it should also be correct to report Peter as realizing that Paderewski is a statesman but as not realizing both that Paderewski is a statesman and that Paderewski is a pianist (it is in this sense that the present version of the puzzle rests essentially on one premise) . However, we now have a contradiction (of the form S & ~(S & T), T & ~(T & S)).

It might be thought that the use of "Paderewski" in the two reports is equivocal – meaning something like "Paderewski the pianist" in the first report and "Paderewski the statesman" in the second. But we may suppose, as before, that the reporter is in the dark about Peter's peculiar situation and so no equivocation in the use of name or shift in the context can plausibly be maintained.

It is evident that the present version of the puzzle does not presuppose Consistency. Nor is it beset by the question of whether there is an unequivocal reading of the belief-sentences. For we are dealing with a single report and it is hardly credible that the readings of the relevant belief-sentences might change mid-way in the course of the report. Thus responses to the puzzle that depend upon questioning Consistency or upon arguing for an equivocation in the sense of "belief" do not plausibly apply in this case.

De re version

Kripke's version of the puzzle has Peter expressing his beliefs with a fractured use of the name "Paderewski" and has us reporting his beliefs with an unfractured use of the name. But there is no need to suppose that Peter has a fractured use of the name or even has any name for Paderewski. For we may suppose that Peter learns that Paderewski is a pianist by hearing him in a concert hall and that he later learns that Paderewski is a statesman by observing him at a political rally, without being aware that he is the same person or even that he is called "Paderewski."

It would then appear to be correct to report Peter as realizing that Paderewski is a pianist but as not realizing both that Paderewski is a pianist and that Paderewski is a statesman. For given that the negative part of the report can indicate Peter's lack of coordinated belief in the previous case, it is unclear why it should not be equally capable of indicating his lack of coordinated belief in the present case, notwithstanding the absence of a shared name. But we can now derive a contradiction, using the symmetric "statesman"-report in the same way as before.

This version of the puzzle differs in some further significant ways from Kripke's. In the first place, what is important about Peter's beliefs is not that they be expressed by means of a fractured name but that they be uncoordinated. Thus, from the present point of view, the use of fractured names in the original presentation is merely a device for making vivid the lack of coordination in Peter's beliefs.

In the second place, the presentation rests upon a de re rather than a purely de dicto understanding of the belief reports since, of course, it would not be correct to report Peter as believing that Paderewski is a pianist (or a statesman) except in a de re sense. This shows that the puzzle does not depend essentially upon adopting a de dicto understanding of belief reports and can arise when the reporter makes no attempt to match the subject's expression of his beliefs with his own. Indeed, there is a way in which the argument might be even stronger under the de re reading of the belief reports, since we no longer have to deal with the worry that Peter's fractured use of the name might prevent us from correctly reporting his beliefs by means of an unfractured use of the name.

In the third place, Disquotation plays no role in the present version of the puzzle. This is an important diagnostic clue, since it suggests that it is not this assumption that is at fault in the original de dicto version of the puzzle.

Quantificational version

In the previous version of the puzzle, we had the reporter use the name "Paderewski," but not the subject. But we need not even assume that the reporter has the use of a name for Paderewski. For surely it is correct (under a suitable reading) to say that there is a famous Pole of whom Peter realizes that he is a pianist but of whom he fails to realize both that he is a pianist and that he is a statesman (in symbols, $\exists x(F(x)$ & Rel[Pianist$(x)]$ & ~(Rel[Pianist$(x)]$ & Rel[Statesman$(x)]$]))), given that Peter realizes that Paderewski is a pianist but has no coordinated belief that he is a statesman. By the same token, it will be correct to say that there is a famous Pole of whom Peter realizes that he is a statesman but of whom he fails to realize both that he is a statesman and a pianist ($\exists x(F(x)$ & Rel[Statesman$(x)]$ & ~(Rel[Statesman$(x)]$ & Rel[Pianist$(x)]$)))). But these two statements together imply that there are at least two famous Poles, which is hardly the way to establish Polish exceptionalism.

Again, this version of the puzzle provides an important diagnostic clue. For variables are devices of reference par excellence and so the fact that the puzzle can arise from the use of variables suggests that there might be a solution to the original puzzle that is compatible with a referential treatment of names.

Belief-free

There is also a variant of Kripke's puzzle that makes no appeal to belief reports or the like. Suppose that Peter is warranted in asserting "Paderewski is a pianist." Knowing that Peter can be trusted on the matter, then surely I am also warranted in asserting "Paderewski is a pianist." Similarly, suppose that Peter is warranted in asserting "Paderewski is a statesman." Then again, knowing that Peter can be trusted on the matter, surely I am also warranted in asserting "Paderewski is a statesman." But if am warranted in making both assertions, then surely I am warranted in drawing the conclusion "Paderewski is both a pianist and a statesman" from them. Yet how can this be given that it goes beyond what Peter, the sole source of my information, was himself willing to assert?

Non-composite

It might be thought that Kripke's puzzle essentially arises from the use of composite reports and the tension between the apparent incorrectness of the composite report and the apparent correctness of the component reports. But this is not so. For suppose that Peter has a belief which he would express in the words "Paderewski is a pianist" (his use of the name is so far unfractured). Sue overhears him and derives her use of the name from his. Then surely she can correctly report Peter as believing that Paderewski is a pianist. But for reasons that will soon become apparent, let us suppose that Sue does not refer to Peter by name but as "the man with jug ears." Thus what she actually says is "the man with jug ears believes that Paderewski is a pianist" (an appellation that Peter fails to recognize as applying to himself). Peter overhears her and, taking her to be referring to another Paderewski, derives what, for him, is another use of the name. Then surely he can use her words and the newly derived use of the name to reproduce what she says; and given that her report is correct, then so is his. Thus he can correctly report that the man with jug ears, viz. Peter, believes that Paderewski [second use] is a pianist. But how can that be since he is only willing to assent to the sentence "Paderewski [first use] is a pianist," and not to the sentence "Paderewski [second use] is a pianist"?[4]

We can also formulate a belief-free version of this form of the puzzle, which is especially simple. Suppose that Peter is warranted in asserting "Paderewski is a pianist" (using an unfractured name) and that Sue overhears what he says. Sue may then derive her use of the name from him and, knowing that he can be trusted on the matter, she will also be warranted in asserting "Paderewski is a pianist." Let us now suppose that Peter overhears what she says and takes her to be referring to a different Paderewski. He may then derive another use of the name from her and, again, knowing that she can be trusted on the matter, he will be warranted in asserting "Paderewski is a pianist." But how can that be, for he is the sole source of the information that is being reproduced and yet, in subsequently asserting "Paderewski is a pianist," he would be going beyond what he himself was originally willing to assert? Of course, essentially the same puzzle would arise if we simply talked of each person "reproducing" what the other person said. It would then appear to follow that Peter reproduced what he originally said, which does not appear to be so!

We should note that the present version of the puzzle is about the first-person reporting of beliefs or the first-person reproduction of content. Thus it shows that the problems raised by the puzzles are not essentially tied to third-person cases of reporting what someone believes or reproducing what they say.

Use and understanding

Suppose that, after picking up his use of the name "Paderewski" for the pianist, Peter says "Paderewski is a pianist." Then he has competently used the name "Paderewski." Similarly, suppose that, after picking up the use of the name "Paderewski" for the statesman, Peter says "Paderewski is a statesman." Then again he has competently used the name. However, he has not competently used the name in the two sentences taken together. But how can that be? How can each individual use be competent but not the joint use?

And analogously for understanding. If I say "Paderewski is a pianist" and Peter takes me to be referring to the pianist, then he has understood my sentence. Similarly, if I say "Paderewski is a statesman" and Peter takes me to be referring to the statesman, then again he has understood my sentence. However, he has not understood both sentences taken together. But how is that possible? How can he properly understand the individual uses but not their joint use?

These variants of the puzzle have significant implications for our understanding of the original puzzle. As I have already mentioned, they provide important diagnostic clues. But they also show that the original puzzle has nothing essential to do with names or with belief reports or with making composite reports or claims and that essentially the same puzzle could have arisen even if names had never been introduced into the language or even if there had existed no linguistic means for describing our beliefs or intentional states. Most solutions to the puzzle target the composite case and take the form of proposing a semantics or pragmatics for the use of names in belief reports. But these solutions cannot be regarded as getting to the heart of the matter unless it is clear how they might extend to the variant puzzles in which the use of names or the reporting of beliefs or the making of composite claims is not in question.

C.   A Response

In relation to any puzzle, one might distinguish between a *response* and a *solution*. A response is merely an indication of where one thinks things have gone wrong (one locates an error either in one of the assumptions from which the contradiction is derived or in the reasoning by which it is derived). A solution, on the other hand, is an attempt to explain or justify the response. It is not evident what response one should make – which is why there is a puzzle; and so for a response to have any credibility, it must receive support from a credible solution.

I wish in the present section to outline a response to the puzzles and to guard it against certain misunderstandings; in the next section, I shall provide a relatively superficial solution to the puzzles; and in the section after that, I shall provide a deeper, more satisfying solution – one that explains away some of the puzzling features of the superficial solution.

What I would like to say, in response to Kripke's original puzzle, is that the report that Peter believes that Paderewski is musical is correct, that the report that Peter believes Paderewski is not musical is also correct, but that the composite report consisting of the two individual reports taken together is not correct. Thus in a situation in which one intends to provide a faithful report of what Peter believes, it would be correct to give either report but it would not be correct to give both (and similarly for the variant puzzles). I am disinclined to draw any distinction between "correctness" and "truth" in the present case and so I would also want to say that the individual belief reports are true while the composite belief report is false.

I believe that this response, at least when stated in terms of correctness, is very intuitive. But a great deal more needs to be said in its defense before it can be considered satisfactory. We should first note that Kripke's formulation of the puzzle does not even provide us with the terms by which this response might be given. This is because he presents the puzzle in the material mode, in terms of what Peter believes, rather than in the formal mode, in terms of the correctness of the belief reports themselves. How we should mold our response to Kripke's own formulation of the puzzle is a delicate matter. Suppose he asks: "does Peter believe that Paderewski is musical?" We should say "yes." He *then* asks: does Peter believe that Paderewski is not musical? Whether we say "yes" or not will depend upon whether we think of the two answers together as constituting two separate reports or as constituting a single composite report.

We, therefore, see that Kripke's presentation of the puzzle may have got in the way of seeing how it should be solved, for it seems to show that a contradiction will follow by impeccable reasoning from the application of the assumptions of Disquotation and Consistency to incontrovertible data; and this naturally leads one to suppose that one should respond to the puzzle by rejecting one or other of those assumptions. But if I am right, there is a problem in the reasoning of the puzzle which cannot be readily discerned from his presentation, since it fails to distinguish between our making two separate belief reports (affirmed on the basis of two applications of Disquotation to the data) and our making a composite belief report (rejected on the basis of Consistency). Thus despite Kripke's great care in making explicit the assumptions upon which the puzzle rests, it is unclear from his formulation where the error in the reasoning of the puzzle is actually to be located.

It might be thought that our response is a form of contextualism. For we may be said to have two separate reports when the context is different and a single composite report when the context is the same. However, there is nothing recognizable here as a difference in context in the usual sense of the term. When Sue holds up one report card, or the other report card, or both, there is no difference in the external circumstances or in her mental state that might be identified as a difference in context. Or rather, the closest we come to such a difference is her intending to make a single composite belief report in the one case but not in the others. But then we must already appeal to the intended notion of context in describing her intention.

The contexts in the relevant sense are "formal" rather than "substantive." They make no further contribution to content; and if one asks "what makes for a difference in the context of two belief reports?," then there is nothing informative one can say unless it is that they are *treated* as different. Contexts, so understood, might be compared to suppositional contexts. Imagine that I suppose that P and that I subsequently suppose that Q. Am I then justified in inferring P & Q? That depends upon whether the suppositional contexts are the same or different, i.e. on whether one is making two separate suppositions or a single composite supposition. But the suppositional context makes no contribution to content; and if one asks "what makes the suppositional contexts different?," there is nothing one can point to beyond the intention to treat them as different.

Contexts, in the relevant sense here, are a kind of scope marker; and the present view is that just as one may have a wider or narrower scope for a sequence of suppositions, so one may have a wider or narrower scope for a sequence of belief reports. However, we do not normally think of assertions as subject to scope. The joint import of two suppositions will depend upon whether we think of them as belonging to the same suppositional context. But how can the joint import of two assertions depend upon whether we think of them as belonging to the same "assertive" context? The fundamental problem we, therefore, face in justifying the present response is to show how scopal distinctions might be relevant to assertion and how, in particular, it is possible for a composite belief report to have some further import beyond the individual reports that make it up, so that it is possible for the composite report to be incorrect when the individual reports themselves are correct.

D.   A Solution

There is a relatively superficial answer to this question that is already implicit in our diagnosis of what was unacceptable about the attribution of contradictory beliefs to Peter (under the heading of "Consistency" in section B). We suggested that what made the attribution unacceptable was the absence of a match in coordination; there was a coordination among the use of the names in the reports that was lacking in the believer's expression of his beliefs. This idea provides the basis for a more general account of the conditions under which a simple or composite belief report will be correct.

Suppose that we make a composite report of someone's beliefs. We say: he believes S_1, he believes S_2, . . . , he believes S_n. Let us also suppose that the person would express the beliefs we are attempting to describe by means of the sentences T_1, T_2, . . . , T_n. To avoid needless complications, we may suppose that, except for the choice of names, he would use the very same words in expressing his beliefs as we use in describing them and that the correctness of the report simply turns on there being an appropriate connection between the sequence of names $M_1, M_2, \ldots, M_k$ that we use in describing his beliefs and the corresponding sequence of names $N_1, N_2, \ldots, N_k$ that he uses in expressing them.

We now ask: under what conditions might the belief report be considered correct? Three answers suggest themselves:

1 *Pure de re reading*: This is the reading under which all that is required for the correctness of the report is that the corresponding names should be coreferential. Under this reading, of course, Kripke's puzzle will not arise since it will clearly be correct to report the person as believing both that Paderewski is musical and that Paderewski is not musical.

2 *Weak de dicto reading*: According to this reading, the correctness of the report will require, in addition, that there should be co-coordination in the use of the names. In other words, the names M_i and M_j of the reporter should be coordinated ($1 \leq i < j \leq k$) just in case the corresponding names N_i and N_j of the believer are coordinated. Note that this answer does not require that the reporter should use the same names as the believer. Suppose, for example, that Paderewski also goes under the name "Fred" and that Peter has two beliefs concerning Paderewski which he would express in the words "Fred is a pianist" and "Fred is a statesman" (with an unfractured use of "Fred"). Then it would be correct to report Peter as believing that Paderewski is a pianist and that Paderewski is a statesman under this reading, since his beliefs are coordinated in the same manner as the report. However, it would not be correct to report Kripke's Peter as having these beliefs under this reading, even though he would be willing to express his beliefs in the words "Paderewski is a pianist" and "Paderewski is a statesman," since the names are not coordinated in the expression of his belief in the manner required by the report.

3 *Strict de dicto reading*: According to this reading, the correctness of the report will not only require co-coordination, i.e. that the *intra*-personal use of the names should be the same, it will also require cross-coordination, i.e. that the *inter*-personal use of the names should be the same. Each of the individual names M_i used by the reporter ($i = 1, 2, \ldots, k$) should be coordinated with the

corresponding name N*i* used by the believer. Under this reading, it would not be correct to report *our* Peter as believing that Paderewski is a pianist or as believing that Paderewski is a statesman, since his use of the name "Fred" in expressing his beliefs would not be coordinated with our use of "Paderewski."

I believe that these different readings are all possible, i.e. that we can make belief reports in conformity with the standards of correctness that they require.[5] Indeed, it seems to me that the de dicto readings and their requirement of co-coordination are especially important for the purposes of psychological explanation. Suppose, for example, that I wish to explain why Peter believes that Paderewski is a Polish pianist. Then my explanation might go as follows: he believes that Paderewski is Polish; he also believes that Paderewski is a pianist; and from these two beliefs he infers that Paderewski is a Polish pianist. But this explanation would be inadequate, as it stands, unless it were presupposed that the two beliefs were appropriately coordinated, i.e. unless the composite belief report was taken to be at least weakly de dicto (and similarly in cases involving belief and desire and the explanation of action). We, therefore, have a strong rationale for taking our belief reports to be at least weakly de dicto and we may also have a rationale for taking them to be strongly de dicto in so far as our focus is on individual interaction rather than individual behavior.

These various readings may now be used to justify some of our response to the puzzle cases. Suppose that we adopt the strict de dicto reading. Then it will presumably be correct to report Kripke's Peter as believing that Paderewski is musical and to report him as believing that Paderewski is not musical. But it will not be correct to report him as believing both that Paderewski is musical and that Paderewski is not musical, since there will not be the required co-coordination between our use the name "Paderewski" in reporting Peter's beliefs and his use of the name in expressing them. Similarly for the "de re" case in which Peter has two "takes" on Paderewski but does not have the use of the name "Paderewski" (section B). If we adopt the weak de dicto reading, it will be correct to report Peter as believing that Paderewski is musical and also to report him as believing that Paderewski is not musical. But it will not be correct to report him as believing both that Paderewski is musical and Paderewski is not musical since, again, there will not be the required co-coordination in the use of the names (or in the reporter's use of the names and Peter's "take" on the objects should he lack any name for Paderewski).

We may illustrate the general character of the above solution by means of an analogy. A mimic may indicate what someone does through imitation. Now it is not essential that he exactly imitate what the other does. If he it to imitate my standing up, for example, it is perhaps not essential that he stand up at the same pace though it is perhaps essential that if I stand up at a uniform pace then he should too. Suppose now that I stand up and sit down at a uniform pace. He may indicate my standing up by standing up at a uniform pace and he may indicate my sitting down by sitting down at a uniform pace. But if the paces at which he stands up and sits down are not the same, then he cannot indicate my standing up and sitting down by putting his acts of standing up and sitting down together, since he thereby indicates that my standing up and sitting down were not at a uniform pace. Belief reports are imitative in somewhat the same way; and just as there may be more to the accuracy of a composite act of mimicry than the accuracy of the individual acts, so may there be more to the correctness of a composite belief report than the correctness of the individual reports.

An analogous response can be given to the puzzles concerning the use and understanding of a name (under "Use and understanding" in section B). For competence in the use of a name requires that different uses of the same name be coordinated and a proper understanding of the use of a name requires that one understand when its different uses are coordinated. It is for this reason that Peter's individual uses of the name "Paderewski" are competent, though not the joint use, and that he understands the individual uses of the name but not the joint use (just as someone could use or understand the variables "x" and "y" individually but not how they work together).

E.   A Deeper Puzzle

Unfortunately, the above solution is not altogether satisfactory as it stands. For one thing, coordination would appear to be a semantic

Figure 4.1   The situation in the de dicto case

phenomenon and so one would like to be able to provide an underlying semantical account of what it is. But more significantly, we need to be assured that the possibilities for coordination required by the readings are genuinely available to us.

Consider the de re puzzle first. Our response takes there be a pair of names M_1, M_2 (of the reporter) and a pair of names N_1, N_2 (which the believer might use in expressing his beliefs) which are such that M_1 is coreferential with N_1, M_2 is coreferential with N_2, M_1 is coordinated with M_2, and yet N_1 is not coordinated with N_2. Now there is no difficulty in recognizing such a possibility if one is a Fregean, since the facts of coreference are compatible with M_1 having the same sense as M_2 and N_1 not having the same sense as N_2. There is, however, a special difficulty for the referentialist. For given the facts of coreference, the semantic role of M_1 and N_1 and of M_2 and N_2 will be the same for him. But then the pairs of names M_1, N_1 and M_2, N_2 will be semantically indistinguishable and so, given that coordination is a semantic phenomenon, how will it be possible to have coordination between M_1 and M_2 but not between N_1 and N_2?

It is at this point that relationism can come to the rescue. For the relationist may grant that M_1 has the same semantic role as N_1 and M_2 the same semantic role as N_2 and yet deny that the pair M_1, M_2 has the same semantic role as the pair N_1, N_2. Indeed, he may take coordination to be strict coreference; and it is then evident that the failure of co-coordination will be compatible with the facts of coreference. Familiar relational strategy will, therefore, enable us to account for our response at the deeper semantical level.

However, the de dicto form of the puzzle raises further difficulties. Our response to the puzzle in this case takes there be a pair of names M_1, M_2 (of the reporter) and a pair of names N_1, N_2 (of the believer) which are such that M_1 is coordinated with N_1, M_2 is coordinated with N_2, M_1 is coordinated with M_2, and yet N_1 is not coordinated with N_2. The situation is as depicted in Figure 4.1, where Peter's fractured use of the name (N_1, N_2) is derived from our unfractured use (M_1, M_2).

But how can this be? For our informal understanding of coordination is as some form of sameness – in meaning or representation. And so how can coordination fail to be transitive? And given that it is transitive, coordination between M_1 and N_1, M_1 and M_2, and M_2 and N_2 will guarantee coordination between N_1 and N_2.[6]

The puzzle in this form can be seen to rest upon two assumptions concerning the conditions under which we have coordination. Let us say that two tokens of a name, when uttered by a single speaker, are *internally linked* just in case the speaker takes them to have the same use and that two tokens of a name, when uttered by different speakers, are *externally linked* just in case the one speaker's use of the first token is directly derived from the other speaker's use of the second token or vice versa. The first of the assumptions states a necessary and sufficient condition for *intra*-personal coordination:

> *Internal link*: When two tokens of a given name are uttered by a single speaker, they will be coordinated if and only if they are internally linked.

The second of the assumptions states a sufficient condition for *inter*-personal coordination:

> *External link*: When two tokens of a given name are uttered by different speakers, they will be coordinated if they are externally linked.

The puzzle can now be seen to arise from a conflict between the two Link principles and:

> *Transitivity*: If M is coordinated with N and N with P, then M is coordinated with P.

For suppose that there are external links between M_1 and N_1 and between M_2 and N_2, an internal link between M_1 and M_2, but no internal link between N_1 and N_2 (these are the incontrovertible data). It will then follow by the Link principles that there is a coordination within the pairs (M_1, N_1), (M_2, N_2) and (M_1, M_2); and so by Transitivity, there will be coordination between N_1 and N_2, contrary to Internal link.

I believe that this is the deepest problem raised by the Kripke-type puzzles. How are we to resolve the conflict between Transitivity and the Link Principles?

F.   A Deeper Solution

If we are to sustain the previous line of solution, then we must reject Transitivity. But how is this even on the cards given that coordination is a form of strict coreference?

In considering this question, it will be convenient to think of coordination not as a relation between tokens of a name but between what one might call *individual uses* of a name. Thus Peter, whose use of the name is fractured, will have two individual uses of the name "Paderewski," while we, whose use is unfractured, will have one individual use of the name. An individual use is, in effect, a way of collecting together internally linked tokens. The question now is: how might it possible for an individual use N_1 be coordinated with N_2 and N_2 with N_3, though not N_1 with N_3.

There is a clue as to how this might be possible in our explanation of the distinction between accidental and strict coreference. We observed that it may be semantically required that "Cicero" refer to the object c and also be semantically required that "Tully" refer to c and yet not be semantically required that the two names refer to the same object, since it might not be manifest that the object c in the two requirements is the same. But, by the same token, might it not be semantically required that the individual use N_1 be coreferential with N_2 and semantically required that N_2 be coreferential with N_3 and yet not semantically required that N_1 be coreferential with N_3, on the grounds that it may not be manifest that the individual use N_2 in the two requirements is the same?

I believe that this line of thought is essentially correct. However, it is in danger of being too restrictive. For we do not, in general, want the role of expressions in semantic requirements to be opaque. Thus, given that a complex expression E is built up in a certain way from the component expressions E_1 and E_2 and given that E_1 and E_2 receive the respective semantic values e_1 and e_2, we need to be able to take for granted that the components of E are the same expressions as those that receive the semantic values if the semantic information is to be of any help in determining a semantic value for E! Compositionality appears to require transparency of expression even if not of semantic value. However, all that it strictly requires – and all that may reasonably be required – is that a semantics for a given language should be transparent with respect to the expressions of that very language.[7] Syntax is transparent, even if semantics is not; and one's take on the expressions of the language should always be presumed to be the same, even if one's take on their referents is not. Thus any failure of the speaker to see two names that are in fact the same as the same should be attributable to a deficiency in his attempt to apply the semantics of the language rather than to a deficiency in the semantics itself.

But such a requirement is perfectly compatible with the semantics being opaque with respect to the expressions of some other language, even when it is in the business of relating the meaning of its own expressions to the meaning of the other expressions. And this, of course, is the situation we face in the present case. For it will be part of the semantics governing Peter's individual uses of the name "Paderewski" that his one individual use should be coreferential with *our* individual use and that his other individual use should also be coreferential with *our* use. Thus there is no need to suppose that the semantics for his two uses of the name should be transparent with respect to our use of the name; and so the inference to its being semantically required that his two uses of the name should be coreferential may be blocked.

Unfortunately, the present proposal is in danger of being too restrictive in a quite different way. For suppose that Peter derives a use P_1 of "Paderewski" from our use P_2 and that another person, call him "Charles," derives a use P_3 of "Paderewski" from our use P_2. We then want P_1 and P_3 to be coordinated and hence strictly coreferential. It should be possible, for example, for Charles to use his name to reproduce what Peter says with *his* name. But how can we get the strict coreference in this case (call it the "Peter/Charles case") but not in the original case (call it the "Peter/Peter case") in which it is the same person, Peter, and not a different person, Charles, who derives P_3 from P_2?

This is a difficult problem and let me briefly indicate how I think it might be solved. In the first place, we should refine our previous account of the semantic relationship between two individual uses of a name when one is derived from the other. Suppose that Peter wishes to derive his use of the name "Paderewski," P_1, from our use, P_2. Then his primary aim is to coordinate his use of the name with what he takes to be the common use of the name. Thus a consequence of

Figure 4.2

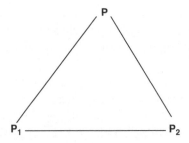

Figure 4.3

his semantic act, if successful, will be that his use P_1 of the name is strictly coreferential with the common use of the name, P. But Peter's access to the common use of the name is through our use of the name and it is, therefore, plausible that the common use of the name, as it figures in his semantics, should be coordinated with the common use of the name, as it figures in ours. Thus the simple situation in Figure 4.2, in which it is taken to be a semantic requirement on Peter's use of the name that it be coreferential with ours is replaced by the more complex situation in Figure 4.3, in which it is a semantic requirement on Peter's and our uses that they be coreferential with what is taken to be a single common use.

It is important, in the second place, to locate the source of the semantic requirements on the individual uses of a name, when different speakers of the language are involved. Consider again the Peter/Charles case (Peter derives P_1 from P_2 while Charles derives P_3 from P_2.) Then whether P_1 is strictly coreferential with P_3 does not simply turn on Peter's semantics or on Charles' but on the two semantics taken together. Thus in order to settle the question of strict coreference in this case we must ascertain which requirements belong to the *joint* semantics.

If we regard the semantics of an individual as a possible body of knowledge possessed by the individual, then we should regard the semantics of a group of individuals as a possible body of knowledge possessed by the group. Thus the question we need to consider is:

given that different individuals know various things then what is it that they *jointly* know? Applying the answer to the special case of a semantics will then tell us what the requirements of a joint semantics should be given the requirements of the individual semantics of which it is composed.

Now it would not normally be thought that there was any difficulty in understanding the notion of joint knowledge. For a group of individuals will know whatever is a logical consequence of what the individuals know. Thus suppose that p_1, p_2, p_3, . . . are the "general pool" of propositions known by at least one individual from the group. Then the propositions known by the group will be the logical consequences of the propositions p_1, p_2, p_3, . . . in the general pool.

However, a peculiar difficulty arises when knowledge of singular propositions is in question. For what the group knows in this case are the *manifest* consequences of the propositions in the general pool; and what the manifest consequences of the proposition are will depend upon the pattern of coordination among them. What then should their pattern of coordination be taken to be?

Now it is clear that the individual patterns of coordination should be preserved within the general pool. If some individual's propositions are coordinated in a certain way, then they should remain coordinated in that way when added to the general pool. But what of propositions that derive from different individuals? Given that they are externally coordinated in a certain way, should it be supposed that they are internally coordinated in this way when added to the pool? Should the external links between the individual minds become internal links within the "group mind" when the barriers between them are removed?

There are different ways of answering this question. The most natural is to adopt an impersonal or "objective" point of view and take each external link to be an internal link. Suppose, for example, that one individual knows that x Fs and another has coordinated knowledge that x Gs. It will then follow on this approach that they can jointly be said to know that x both Fs and Gs.

However, this approach gives rise to a further difficulty. For suppose that I have some fractured knowledge concerning x. I know that x Fs and also have some uncoordinated knowledge that x Gs. Suppose also that my knowledge that x Fs and my knowledge that x Gs are both externally coordinated with your knowledge that x Hs.

If these external links become internal links, it will then follow (given that coordination is an equivalence relation) that my two occurrences of x will become coordinated. Thus the perspective of the group mind, as given by its internal links, will not be compatible with the perspective of each individual mind.

In order to avoid this difficulty, we might adopt a personal or "subjective" point of view and refuse to let any of the external links become an internal link. The external links would not then be relevant to what we jointly know and, in particular, we would not be able to conclude, in the example above, that we jointly know that x both Fs and Gs.

Neither of these approaches is what we are after in the case of semantics. The first is too broad, since it will imply that P_1 is strictly coreferential with P_3 in the Peter/Peter case.[8] The second is too narrow, since it will fail to imply that P_1 is strictly coreferential with P_3 in the Peter/Charles case.

There is, however, an intermediate approach. Under what one might call the inter-subjective approach, we adopt the objective perspective to the extent that it is compatible with the subjective perspective of each individual. In other words, we attempt to retain as much in the way of external coordination as we can while respecting the internal coordination of each individual. Or to put the matter more formally, we might say that a coordination-scheme on the general pool of propositions is *inter-subjectively acceptable* if it agrees with the coordination-scheme on each individual body of propositions. We will then jointly know whatever we know under some inter-subjectively acceptable coordination-scheme.

It is the inter-subjective approach that will provide us with the required semantic underpinning for our judgments of coordination in the puzzle cases. Thus, in the Peter/Peter case, we will deny that P_1 is strictly coreferential with P_3, for the only way to reach this conclusion is to coordinate the occurrences of the common use, P, that are tied to P_1, P_2 and P_3, thereby going against the lack of coordination between the occurrences tied to P_1 and P_3 within Peter's own semantics. On the other hand, in the Peter/Charles case, we can accept that P_1 is strictly coreferential with P_3 since all of the different occurrences of the common use can be coordinated without going against the pattern of coordination within any given individual's semantics.

The solution can be generalized. Let us say that a sequence M_1, $M_2, \ldots, M_k$, $k \geq 1$, of individual uses of a name is a *referential path from* M *to* N if $M = M_1$, $N = M_k$, and, for each $i = 1, 2, \ldots, k - 1$, M_i is directly derived from M_{i+1} or M_{i+1} is directly derived from M_i. Referential paths provide the route by which a name is transmitted from one speaker to another. Let us now say that such a path is *coherent* if no two distinct individual uses M_i and M_j on the path, for $1 \leq i < j \leq k$, belong to the same individual. Thus a coherent referential path is one that respects each individual's perspective on his use of the individual names. The name M can then be taken to be *inter-subjectively* coordinated with the name N if there is a coherent referential path from the one to the other. Using this notion of coordination in our account of the de dicto readings (along with the corresponding notion of coordination for a *sequence* of individual uses) enables us to provide a solution to all possible puzzle cases.[9]

There are two aspects of the present approach worthy of note. In the first place, it is essentially semantic in character. Intentions may serve to fix a reading of a belief report. But once given a reading, the correctness of a belief report is then simply a question of there being an appropriate semantic match between the sentence used in reporting the belief and the sentence that might be used in expressing the belief; and the basic semantical apparatus of referentialism, once reconfigured along relational lines, is sufficient to provide us with the resources by which the peculiar features of the semantic matching may be understood. It was never very plausible that the puzzles were pragmatic in origin; and it was perhaps only a tendency to see context as an all-purpose "hidden variable" of linguistic explanation that originally led philosophers to think that it might be relevant in the present case.

In the second place, our response to the puzzles involves a subtle interplay between various subjective, inter-subjective, and objective elements of language (which are no doubt typical to some extent of all forms of conventional behavior). We have, on the one hand, a language in common use, such as English, and we have, on the other hand, the particular versions of that language that have been adopted by its speakers. Often these will come apart, as when Peter has two use of the name "Paderewski" for the famous Polish pianist where the common language has only one. However, the individual versions of the language – at least, in regard to the behavior of proper names

– are to be understood by reference to the common language. Thus the basic semantic rule for each of Peter's two uses of the name "Paderewski" is that it should be coreferential with the use of the name in the common language. This is a reflection of the basic fact that, in speaking a language, we are attempting to speak the common language. It does not just so happen that we end up speaking languages that are more or less alike, but it is built into the very semantics of the language we speak that its expressions – or, at least, its proper names – should mean what is commonly meant.

But there is also a sense in which the common language should be understood by reference to the individual versions of the common language. For the common use of a proper name is a product, so to speak, of the individual uses of the name. It stretches as far as, and no further than, the internal and external links by which the individual uses of the name are given. There is a kind of circularity here and it is perhaps a deep question to say in exactly what it consists. But it would at least appear to be relatively unproblematic in the present case, since there would appear to be no essential difficulty in supposing that the common use of the name, by which we coordinate our own use of the name, should itself be constituted by such uses.

In addition to the common language and the various individual languages is what one might call the "communal" language. Like the common language, it is a product of the various individual languages, but it is an "inner" rather than an "outer" product. Each individual language constitutes a more or less accurate perspective on the common language and, in forming a joint perspective on the common language, we may attempt to be faithful to the idiosyncrasies of each individual perspective, thereby obtaining something more richly variegated and more individualistic than the common language itself. The resulting language is a kind of "quilt," stitched together from the "pieces" of individual language in such as way as to retain their individual character.

The common language is, in a sense, objective; it is not tied to the perspective of individual speakers. The individual languages, by contrast, are subjective and merely reflect a given speaker's perspective. The communal language, in contrast to both of these, is intersubjective; it reflects the perspective of individual speakers, but not the perspective of one speaker as opposed to another.

The common language is the one we attempt to speak in representing the world. But we do not always succeed and the way we represent the world is not then an accurate reflection of how our common language represents the world. When this is so, it is the communal, rather than the common, language that is best suited to understanding how we represent the world. For it provides us with the means of describing what someone else believes while still being faithful to the way we represent our own beliefs. It is perhaps one of the more surprising lessons of the puzzles that they point to the need for this intermediate level of representation, lying between the common language and the idiolects of individual speakers.

G.   The Role of Variables in Belief Reports

I have presented a solution to the de dicto and de re forms of the puzzle but still have not dealt with the quantificational version (introduced in section B). We would like to report Peter as believing (or realizing) of some famous Pole that he is a pianist but not as believing (or realizing) both that he is a pianist and that he is a statesman. In symbols:

1   $\exists x[F(x) \ \& \ Bel[P(x)] \ \& \ \sim(Bel[P(x)] \ \& \ Bel[S(x)])]$.

Similarly, we would like to report Peter as believing of some famous Pole that he is a statesman but not as believing both that he is a statesman and that he is a pianist. In symbols:

2   $\exists x[F(x) \ \& \ Bel[S(x)] \ \& \ \sim(Bel[S(x)] \ \& \ Bel[P(x)])]$.

But it follows by classical logic from (1) and (2) that there are at least two famous Poles:

3   $\exists x \exists y(x \neq y \ \& \ F(x) \ \& \ F(y))$,

which is clearly not our intention (and, indeed, if "famous Pole" were replaced by a description true of Paderewski alone, our reports would be inconsistent with the facts).

In this case, there would appear to be no possibility of distinguishing between the correctness of the composite report and the correctness of the component reports. And so what are we to do? Give up classical logic? Or give up on the reports?

The previous relational treatment of variables, when combined with the present account of belief reports, enables us to come up with a remarkable solution to this version of the puzzle – one in which we may affirm both reports while still holding on to a standard objectual interpretation of the quantifiers. For suppose that we attempt to evaluate (1). (1) will be true just in case $F(x)$ & $Bel[P(x)]$ & ~$(Bel[P(x)]$ & $B[S(x)])$ is true for some value of x. However, under the relational semantics, the quantifier $\exists x$ will leave a trace of its binding in terms of a coordination-scheme linking each of the four occurrences of x. The question, therefore, is whether the resulting *coordinated* formula is true for some value of x.

Now, in strict analogy to our account of the role of names in belief reports, it may be supposed that, for the coordinated formula $Bel[P(x)]$ & $B[S(x)]$ to be true of some object x, Peter must have *coordinated* beliefs that the object is a pianist and that it is a statesman. But since Peter does not have such coordinated beliefs when the object is Paderewski, although he does have the de re belief that Paderewski is a pianist, we may conclude that the coordinated formula $F(x)$ & $B[P(x)]$ & ~$(B[P(x)]$ & $B[S(x)])$ is true when x is Paderewski and hence that the existential generalization (1) is true. By the same token, (2) is also true and by virtue of the very same value for x. Thus (1) and (2) may be true and (3) false – in violation of classical logic!

It should be emphasized that the clauses for the basic belief attributions will be relational under the present semantics. It is not, in general, sufficient to consider the truth-value of a belief formula $Bel[A]$ on its own, but only in the context of other belief formulas with which it might be coordinated. Thus the doxastic operator Bel cannot be regarded as a straightforward sentential operator. Syntactically, it applies to sentences but, at the deepest semantic level, it picks out a coordinated body of opinion rather than an uncoordinated range of individual opinions; and it is by reference to this coordinated body of opinion, rather than the individual opinions, that its application must be determined.[10]

The present semantics enables us to repair a serious deficiency in the usual symbolism of quantified doxastic logic (and of quantified logics for the other propositional attitudes). For within such a symbolism, one would like to be able to express the distinction between having the coordinated belief that Cicero is a Roman and that Cicero is an orator, say, and having the (possibly) uncoordinated belief that Cicero is a Roman and that Cicero is an orator. If c is a constant for Cicero, then one naturally expresses this distinction by means of the formulae:

1   $\exists x(x = c \ \& \ Bel[R(x)]) \ \& \ \exists x(x = c \ \& \ Bel[O(x)])$ (there is some individual identical to Cicero that the person believes is a Roman and there is some person identical to Cicero that the person believes is an orator);
2   $\exists x(x = c \ \& \ Bel[R(x)] \ \& \ Bel[O(x)])$ (there is some individual identical to Cicero that the person believes to be a Roman and believes to be an orator).

But these two formulae are equivalent within the standard objectual semantics; and it is hard to see how else to express the distinction unless one implicitly takes the quantifiers to range over senses or "guises" as well as objects. However, by going relational, we can accept the natural formulation of the distinction in terms of these formulae while still holding on to an objectual interpretation of the quantifiers. The present proposal is, therefore, no mere oddity; it probably constitutes the most useful way of developing a quantified logic for the propositional attitudes within an objectual framework for the quantifiers.[11]

H.   Some Semantical Morals

Our approach to Kripke's puzzle has some general implications for a number of different topics – the defense of Referentialism, the semantics of belief reports, and the nature of logical validity – which we now consider.

The puzzles, for Kripke, were meant to serve a larger dialectical purpose. Referentialism, to which Kripke is sympathetic, appears to imply Substitutivity, i.e., the substitutivity, salve veritate, of coreferential names. But Substitutivity appears to have certain counterintuitive consequences in its application to belief reports for, given that Tom believes that Cicero is an orator, Substitutivity implies that Tom also believes that Tully is an orator, which we can easily imagine not to be so. And this suggests that Referentialism should be relinquished.

But what is it about the imagined scenario, Kripke asks, which makes us think that Tom believes that Cicero is an orator but not that Tully is an orator? Surely, it is that Tom is willing to assent to the sentence "Cicero is an orator" and yet not willing to assent to the sentence "Tully is an orator." Thus it is only Substitutivity *in conjunction with* the incontrovertible data concerning assent, the assumption that someone believes that S if he is prepared to assent to S (Disquotation), and the assumption that someone does not believe that S if he is not prepared to assent to S (Converse Disquotation) that creates any difficulty. But what the puzzles then show is that Disquotation is capable of leading to certain counter-intuitive belief attributions on its own, without the benefit of Substitutivity. This, therefore, suggests that it is not Substitutivity which is at fault in the standard examples presented against Referentialism, but Disquotation, and that it is no mark against Referentialism that it should have Substitutivity as a consequence.

This line of response is highly speculative and it is hard to believe that the problematic character of the application of Disquotation in the puzzle cases could serve to throw any doubt on its application in the cases that are used in the standard counter-examples against Referentialism (this is as if we were to give up the theory of transfinite cardinals in response to the set-theoretic paradoxes). I wish to draw a somewhat different moral from the puzzles. For our proposed solution will respect the application of the Disquotation Principles in the usual cases and so it will not enable us to hang on to Substitutivity.[12] However, we are not thereby obliged to give up Referentialism. For just as it is only Substitutivity in conjunction with the Disquotation Principles that created the original difficulties, so it is only Referentialism in conjunction with some form of Intrinsicalism that leads to Substitutivity. Thus by giving up Intrinsicalism, we may accept the counter-examples to Substitutivity and yet still hang on to Referentialism.

Kripke regarded the puzzle in a defensive light, as serving to undermine one of the standard objections to the referentialist position. But our solution to the puzzle enables us to regard it in a more offensive light, as actually posing a *special* difficulty for the Fregean. For consider again the case in which we derive our use P_2 of "Paderewski" from Peter's use P_1 and Peter then derives another use P_3 of the name from our use P_2. If Peter says "P_1 is musical," then we may reproduce what Peter says by saying "P_2 is musical," and Peter, in his turn, may reproduce what we say by saying "P_3 is musical." But Peter does not thereby reproduce what he originally said. To account for this phenomenon, we need a notion of "same-saying" or of "reproducing content" that can fail to be transitive. This is something that the relationist can provide in his notion of *strictly* co-referring or saying the same when the relata between which the relation holds may to some extent be opaque. But it is a mystery what the Fregean might put in its place. If coordination is a matter of having a common sense or "guise" then it must be transitive; and although it might be taken to be some kind of "approximate" identity in sense, it is hard to see how anything of this sort might be relevant in the present case.

We should note, finally, that the failure of transitivity has some radical implications for the conception of logical validity and for the semantics of belief reports. We have already noted that classical logic may fail under a natural semantics for quantified belief reports. But the very idea of validity in virtue of logical form, as this is normally conceived, may also break down. For inference is not merely an intrapersonal matter; it may proceed from speaker to speaker. Thus if you assert P and P $\supset$ Q then I may infer Q from what you said (this sort of thing often goes on – or is what we wish went on – in the logic classroom). Now consider a Peter-Peter case. Peter asserts "Paderewski is musical"; and we, deriving our use of the name from him, may validly infer "Paderewski is musical." But Peter, deriving what he takes to be a new use of the name from us, may then infer "Paderewski is musical." We naturally think of each of these inferences as being valid in virtue of their logic form, viz.:

$$
\frac{P}{P}
$$

and, at the very least, this means that any inference of this form will be valid. Now given that the two inferences are both of this form and given that the conclusion of the first inference is identical to the premise of the second, it follows that the inference from Peter's initial assertion of "Paderewski is musical" to his subsequent assertion of the sentence is also valid. But it is not! Peter could legitimately be accused of making a logical error if he performed such an inference. We, therefore, see that, in special cases of this sort, validity cannot be regarded as a matter of logical form.

If we are correctly to represent the "logical form" in these cases we must use coordinative links. Thus the logical form of the single inferences will be:

$$\begin{array}{c} P \\ \hline P \end{array} \Big]$$

with an explicit line of coordination between premise and conclusion, while the logical form of the chained inference will be:

with two separate lines of coordination between the premise and the middle term and the middle term and the conclusion. An inference of this form is to be distinguished from one of the form:

$$\begin{array}{c} P \\ \hline P \\ \hline P \end{array} \Big]$$

in which premise, middle term, and conclusion are all coordinated. The second of these last two, which corresponds to the normal case, is valid while the first is not.[13]

The implications for the semantics of belief-reports are equally far-reaching. We have already seen that the correctness (or truth) of a composite belief report cannot be taken to turn on whether the individual believes the propositions signified by the embedded clauses of the individual belief reports. But the correctness of a *single* belief report also cannot be taken to turn on whether the subject believes the proposition signified by the embedded clause of the report. For consider the Peter-Peter case; and suppose that Peter has a belief which he would express in the words "P_1 is musical." We may then correctly report Peter as believing that P_2 is musical; and so "P_2 is musical" should express the same proposition as "P_1 is musical." Suppose now that we have a belief which we would express in the words "P_2 is musical." Peter may then correctly report us as believing that P_3 is musical; and so "P_3 is musical" should express the same proposition as "P_2 is musical." But given that "P_1 is musical" and "P_3 is musical" express the same proposition, it should be correct for Peter to report himself as believing that P_3 is musical – which is not so, at least under the intended de dicto reading of the belief reports.

Nothing in this reasoning turns on what we take the proposition to be. It could be linguistic or partly linguistic; it could involve guises or modes of presentation in addition to objects; and it could be tied to the historical facts concerning the origin of the name. The point is that the notion of proposition is simply incapable of playing the *formal* role that these cases impose upon it: for given that the required form of matching is not transitive, it cannot be understood in terms of the possession of a common factor, whatever that common factor might be. Kripke (1979, p. 135) has suggested that the puzzle subjects "the notion of the *content* of someone's assertion, the *proposition* it expresses . . . to the greatest possible strain, perhaps to the point of breakdown." Our treatment of the puzzles indicates that this suggestion is essentially correct and that there are therefore enormous difficulties in providing anything like a standard compositional semantics for individual belief reports.

Postscript: Further Work

I should like, in conclusion, to mention a number of topics that arise from the semantic framework we have developed and that are perhaps worthy of further investigation. I begin with the notion of a *relative* semantic requirement and show how it might have useful application in understanding the nature of anaphor and demonstrative reference, the semantics of tokens and occurrences, and the systematic character of compositionality. I then discuss various features that are desirable in a semantics: it should be capable of dealing with empty reference and other forms of semantic defect; it should explicitly talk about what is or is not semantically required; and it should be open to stipulation. Finally, I consider some ways in which the relational approach is able to throw light on Mates' puzzle and Moore's paradox of analysis.

One-way coordination

Coordination has so far been treated as a two-way affair; if an expression E is coordinated with F then F is also coordinated with E. But many cases of interest are ones in which a given expression *derives* its reference from the reference of another, though not vice versa. The most obvious case is anaphora. In "I met John, he was sporting a fake moustache," the two terms "John" and "he" are strictly coreferential – but "he" derives its reference from "John," not "John" from "he."

How is derived or "anaphoric" reference is to be understood? We took strict coreference to consist in the semantic requirement that the reference of two expressions should be the same. But what of derived reference? I would like to suggest that just as there can be semantic requirements simpliciter so there can be semantic requirements *on* an expression or expressions. To say that the semantic requirement is *on* certain expressions is not to say simply that it concerns them but also that it holds *in virtue of* their meaning or semantic features; it concerns them as *source* rather than simply as *subject*. Suppose, for example, that I introduce "Charlie" as a name for the name "Cicero." Then it is semantically required that "Charlie" names "Cicero." But this is a semantic requirement on "Charlie" in the relevant sense, not on "Cicero"; for even though the requirement concerns both "Charlie" and "Cicero," it is in virtue of "Charlie" meaning what it does, not of "Cicero" meaning what it does, that the requirement holds.[1]

We might now say that one expression *derives* its reference from another if it is a semantic requirement on the first that it should be coreferential with the second.[2] It is then plausible that "he" in the above example can be said to derive its reference from "John," though not "John" from "he."

Relative semantic requirements are subject to a principle of "chaining."[3] Suppose that it is a semantic requirement on the expression E that it be related in a certain way R to the expression F and also suppose that it is a semantic requirement on F that it have a certain feature Q. Then it will be a semantic requirement on E not only that it be related by R to F but also that it be related by R to a term F with the feature Q. In other words, the content of the requirement on F can be "imported" into the content of the requirement on F. With semantic requirements simpliciter, importation can proceed indiscriminately – if it is a semantic requirement both that S and that T it will be a semantic requirement that both S and T. But with relative semantic requirements, importation must be mediated through an appropriate "middle term."

A simple illustration of Chaining is provided by our example of the pronoun "he." It is a semantic requirement on "he" that it should be coreferential with "John" and a semantic requirement on "John" that it should refer to John. By Chaining, it will be a semantic requirement on "he" that it should refer to a name "John" that refers to John and hence, by Closure, it will be a semantic requirement on "he" that it refer to John. The referential features of "John" are thereby transferred to "he."

Indexicals

It is my view that the demonstrative uses of an indexical expression, such as "this" or "it," should be taken to be anaphoric on an associated demonstration. In other words, it should be taken to be a semantic requirement on the use of the indexical that it be coreferential with the demonstration. When the demonstration is private (as with the act of attending to a particular object), this will yield coordination between a given individual's singular thoughts and his use of language. When the demonstration is public (as with the act of pointing to an object in common view), it will yield coordination between different individual uses of the indexical, since each use will be tied to the same demonstration. One striking advantage of this approach is that it makes the deictic uses of an indexical uniform with the intra-linguistic uses.

An especially interesting application of the view is to the first-person pronoun. Let it be granted that certain experiences are of oneself (these may be of a quite ordinary sort). The standard uses of the first person pronoun may then be taken to be anaphoric on such experiences. In other words, it will be a semantic requirement on the use of the first person pronoun that it should be coreferential with an experience of oneself. Thus someone who used the first-person pronoun to refer to a person who in fact was himself but who was identified by purely external means (and even as "the speaker of a given utterance") could not be said to have made a proper use of the word. The usual way of stating the semantics for "I" does not make clear the peculiar way in which the user of the pronoun should identify its referent.

Types, tokens, and occurrences

We may distinguish in a familiar way between type and token expressions. Thus the abstract sentence-type "Cicero is Cicero" (for a given use of the name "Cicero") will have various concrete instances or "tokens." We should also distinguish between occurrences and tokens. Thus the sentence-type "Cicero is Cicero" contains two *occurrences* of the name-type, while a token of the sentence-type will contain two corresponding *tokens* of the name-type.

I believe that there is subtle interplay between the semantic behavior of types, tokens, and occurrences that has not been properly explored and that can only be properly understood with the help of relational ideas. Consider a token of "Cicero is Cicero," by way of example. Its semantic value, I would like to suggest, should be taken to derive from the semantic value of the corresponding type. Thus semantics first operates at the abstract level of types and is then projected downwards to tokens. But how is the semantic value of the type to be determined? Its semantic value, I would like to suggest, should be taken to derive, in part, from the semantic value of the two *occurrences* of the name. In other words, the semantic values of a complex expression-type should be projected upwards from the semantic values of the component occurrences. But what then of the semantic values of the occurrences? These, in their turn, should be projected downwards from the semantic values of the corresponding expression-types.

The relation of "deriving from" to which I have appealed in these explanations should be understood as a form of anaphora. Thus the occurrence of an expression should be taken to be anaphoric on the type – it is to be a semantic requirement on the occurrence that it receive the same semantic value as the type. It is somewhat similar in the case of tokens, though here I think the token derives its *identity* from being anaphoric on the type and not merely its reference.

Semantics is usually pursued at the level of types. But it should be clear that bringing in occurrences and tokens leads to many interesting questions and enables us to give a much more refined description of the semantic facts and the flow of semantic information.

Complex expressions

Something analogous to anaphor can hold between a complex expression and its constituents. Consider the expression "even prime" by way of illustration and let us suppose, merely to fix our ideas, that "even prime" signifies the set of even prime numbers, "even" the set of even numbers and "prime" the set of prime numbers. Then just as it is a semantic requirement on "he" that it should be coreferential with "John," so it will be a semantic requirement on "even prime" that it should signify the intersection of the sets signified by "even" and by "prime."

Given that it is a semantic requirement on "even" that it should signify the set of even numbers and a semantic requirement on "prime" that it should signify the set of prime numbers, we can use Chaining (and Closure) to show that it is a semantic requirement on "even prime" that it should signify the set of even primes. This case, therefore, provides us with a simple model of how a compositional semantics might be taken to proceed within the current framework. It will be a semantic requirement on complex expressions that they be related in a certain way to their immediate constituents; and it will be a semantic requirement on simple expressions that they be related in a certain way to the "world." By making successive applications of Chaining, we can then show how it is a semantic requirement on the complex expressions that they be related in an appropriate way to the world. Thus Chaining becomes the recursive engine, so to speak, through which language acquires its content.

Empty names

I have said little about empty reference, in which the intended referent of a name does not exist, or about "confused" reference, in which two uses of a name are taken to be one. These are both cases of a "defective" semantics, in which the requirements laid down for the use of an expression cannot be met. My inclination is to say that, in such cases, a "backup" semantics comes into effect; given that the original requirements cannot be met, they are replaced with suitably related requirements which can be met. Thus instead of failed reference to an ordinary object, we have successful reference to an intentional object; and instead of failed reference to two ordinary objects, we have successful reference to some sort of amalgam of these objects.

If we are adequately to describe the functioning of a defective semantics, then we need some way to distinguish between the case in which an unsuccessful attempt is made to lay down a semantic requirement and the case in which no attempt is even made. Our previous notion of semantic requirement is of no help in this regard since no semantic requirements are laid down in either case. But we might appeal instead to the notion of a *putative* requirement. We can then say that there is putative semantic requirement in the one case though not in the other.

The putative requirement that S may succeed, in which case it will result in a "genuine" requirement that S, or it may fail, in which case it will be subject to a "back-up" requirement that S', where S' is suitably related to S. If the putative requirement that S fails then it will not be a genuine requirement that S and usually it will not even be the case that S. It will, therefore, be impossible for the speaker to know that S, although he may know that it is a putative semantic requirement that S and he may also know, if he is sufficiently enlightened, that it is a genuine semantic requirement that S'.

The notion of a putative semantic requirement should be of some help in accounting for the incoherent use of language. Some philosophers have supposed, for example, that the Liar Paradox is built into our very understanding of the truth-predicate. This can hardly be taken to mean that it is a semantic requirement that the Liar biconditional should hold, since it would then have to hold in fact. But it could be taken to mean that it is a *putative* requirement that the Liar biconditional should hold; and, given that the requirement cannot be met, there would then arise the question of what the coherent "back-up" requirement should be.

Semantics as reflexive

Terms such as "refers" or "expresses" are clearly semantic and signify relations that may be part of the content of semantic requirements. But what of the term "semantic requirement" itself? Is it also semantic?

I am inclined to think that it is. One fairly compelling reason is that judgments as to what is or is not a semantic requirement would appear to be implicated in our use of language and not merely in the classification of the requirements to which it should conform. For example, it is semantic requirement (one that every competent speaker should be in a position to recognize) that in a proper use of the sentence "Bruce likes him," the pronoun "him" should not be anaphoric on the subject-term "Bruce" (which is not to exclude the possibility that the two terms might co-refer). But anaphora is a matter of strict coreference, of what is semantically required; and so what this in effect amounts to is that it is semantically required that it *not* be semantically required that the pronoun be coreferential with the subject-term. Thus the notion of being semantically required must itself appear as part of the content of what is semantically required.

Given that the notion of being semantically required is itself a semantic notion, it seems reasonable to assume that the notion conforms to the characteristic S4 axiom:

> If it is semantically required that S then it is a semantically required that it is semantically required that S.

It is also not unreasonable to assume the characteristic S5 axiom:

> If it is not semantically required that S then it is a semantically required that it is not semantically required that S,

at least as long as the sentence S in question is itself purely semantic in content. Thus we may conceive of a semantic theory as being embedded in an S5-type logic for the notion of being a semantic requirement (and for a K5-type logic for the notion of being a putative semantic requirement).

The question of the semantic status of the notion of being a semantic requirement is of some relevance to the question of how the doctrine of semantic relationism should be formulated. For we wanted there to be a semantic relationship between two names, viz. strict coreference, that did not hold in virtue of their intrinsic semantic features. But this is to presuppose that the notion of being semantically required should itself be a semantical notion. If this presupposition were to fail, then some other way of formulating the general doctrine would have to be found.

Semantics as the product of stipulation

There is an obvious way in which semantic requirements should be independent of matters of fact. If, for example, it is a semantic requirement that "bachelor" is true of all and only unmarried men then it cannot also be a semantic requirement that "bachelor" is true of all and only unmarried women, since it would then follow that every unmarried man was an unmarried woman. But how is this independence from matters of fact or what is already given to be achieved, and what is it in the nature of a semantics that will guarantee that it obtains?

I believe that the answer rests upon the possibility of being able to regard any (non-defective) semantics as the product of stipulation. This is not to say that it actually is the product of stipulation. The thought, rather, is that it should be possible so to structure the requirements of the semantics that each of them can be seen to arise from a legitimate act of stipulation – one that, by its very nature, will be independent of what might already hold. A well-ordered series of explicit definitions of one term by means of others provides an obvious means by which such independence might be achieved but I suspect that, in order to make sense of the full range of possible semantics, we will need to work with a much broader conception of what might legitimately be stipulated and of how the required independence from what is already given might thereby be achieved.[4]

Mates' puzzle

Let us suppose, if only for the sake of argument, that "doctor" and "physician" are synonyms. It then seems perfectly possible that the sentence "I believe that no one doubts that doctors are doctors" is true and yet the sentence "I believe that no one doubts that doctors are physicians" is false. But how can this be if the terms "doctor" and "physician" are synonyms? This is Mates' puzzle (Mates, 1972).

One might attempt to account for the difference in the truth-value of these sentences by appeal to a difference in the terms. This difference could be semantic. Thus it might be thought that even though the terms have the same "first-order" sense, the "second-order" sense, i.e. the way the first-order sense is presented, is not the same and that it is the second-order sense that is relevant to the truth of the belief-reports. Or the difference could be taken to be a difference in the terms themselves as long as the belief-reports were taken to relate the believer to the sentences themselves rather than to what they express.

There is, however, a version of the puzzle that is resistant to responses of this sort. Suppose that an eccentric professor has made a number of long higgledy-piggledy stipulations. He stipulates that a glub is something that is either a perfect square or a quasar or a monkey's tail . . . , that a frix is something that is either a limit ordinal or a black hole or a pig's nose . . . , and so on; and let us suppose that his students and I have mastered all of these terms in that we are able to reproduce the definitions (and understand the terms by which they have been defined). Let us also suppose that some of these terms, say "glub" and "flox," have been stipulated to have the very same definition but that some of us are not explicitly aware of this fact and may even believe that each term has been given a different definition. Then surely it is possible for the sentence "I believe that no one doubts that glubs are glubs" to be true even though the sentence "I believe that no one doubts that glubs are floxes" is false.

In this case it is impossible to appeal to a semantic difference to explain the difference in truth-value since "glub" and "flox" have been given exactly the same definition. Indeed, we may modify the example so that an appeal to a difference in the terms themselves is also not in order. For let us suppose that the professor stipulates two meanings for each term (perhaps far apart in the order of stipulation) and that I and the students dutifully learn each meaning. Now it may be that the two meanings for the term "glub" are the same but that some of the students are not aware of this fact and may even believe that each term has two different meanings. Then surely it is possible for the sentence "I believe that no one doubts that glubs [one use] are glubs [same use]" to be true even though the sentence "I believe that no one doubts that glubs [one use] are glubs [other use]" is false.

A variant of this case may be used to pose an especially intractable version of Frege's puzzle. For the sentence "glubs are floxes" may be informative to a student in the first of the two examples, even though the sentence "glubs are glubs" is not; and similarly, the sentence "glubs are glubs" may be informative to a student under an equivocal reading of "glub" in the second of the two examples, even though that sentence is not informative under an unequivocal reading.

How is the Fregean to account for the cognitive difference in these cases? Since he appeals to sense to account for the difference in the original version of the puzzle, one might have thought that he could appeal to second-order sense to account for the difference in the present version. But the cases have been constructed in such a way that there is no second-order difference in sense! The Fregean has been hoisted by his own petard; he faces the very same difficulties at the level of sense as he posed for the Referentialist at the level of reference.

These difficulties can be made to disappear under the relational approach. What we must do is find a semantic difference, not between the individual terms "glub" and "flox" (or between the two uses of "glub"), but between the pair of terms "glub", "glub" and the pair of terms "glub", "flox." This suggests, by analogy with the referential case, that we should take it to be a semantic requirement that "glub" is coextensive with "glub" and yet not a semantic requirement that "glub" is coextensive with "flox."

However, the truth of this latter claim is not so clear. For it will presumably be a semantic requirement that "glub" is true of all and only those things that are perfect squares or quasars or monkey's tails . . . Similarly, it will be semantic requirement that "flox" is true of all and only those things that are perfect squares or quasars or monkey's tails . . . But from this it then follows (using only closure under manifest consequence) that it is a semantic requirement that "glub" and "flox" are coextensive.

Thus appeal to the straight notion of semantic requirement is of no help in accounting for the semantic difference between the two pairs of terms. But we can appeal instead to the relative notion. For it is a semantic requirement on "glub" that "glub" is coextensive with "glub" and yet not a semantic requirement on "glub" (but only on "glub" and "flox" taken together) that "glub" is coextensive with "flox." Thus coordination in extension derives from the meaning of the one term in the case of the pair "glub", "glub" but only from the meaning of both terms in the case of the pair "glub", "flox."

Moore's paradox of analysis

We might state Moore's paradox in the following form: given that "brother" and "male sibling" are synonymous, how is it possible for "brothers are male siblings" to be informative (as an account of what it is to be a brother) even though "brothers are brothers" is not? As with Mates' puzzle, philosophers have been tempted to account for the cognitive difference in the sentences by appeal to a difference in the terms "brother" and "male sibling," where this is either a subtle difference in meaning, such as "second-order" sense, or a difference in the terms themselves.

But it is not plausible to suppose that the difference is in the terms themselves, for my intent in saying "brothers are male siblings" is not to say something about the word "brother" but something about what it is to be a brother. The suggestion that there is a subtle difference in meaning is more plausible, especially if I did not acquire the term "brother" by means of an explicit definition. However, a version of Moore's paradox also arises for stipulated terms, such as "glub" and "flox." The sentence "glubs are perfect squares or quasars or monkey's tails . . ." can be informative for someone who understands the term "glub" in a way in which "glubs are glubs" is not. But in such a case it is very hard to say in what the subtle difference in meaning should be taken to consist.

Again, relationism can come to the rescue. For there will be a difference in meaning between the pairs "glub", "glub" and "glub", "perfect square or . . ." in that it will be a semantic requirement on "glub" that it be coextensive with "glub" but not a semantic requirement on "perfect square or . . ." that it be coextensive with "glub." In many cases, it will also be possible to identify an *intrinsic* difference in meaning between the two terms. Let us suppose that "male" signifies the concept *male*, "sibling" the concept *sibling*, and "male sibling" the concept *male-sibling*. It will then be a semantic requirement on "male sibling" that it should signify the conjunction of the concepts *male* and *sibling*. In other words, the concept *male-sibling* will figure in the requirement as the conjunction of two other concepts. However, it is not a semantic requirement on "brother" that it should signify the conjunction of *male* and *sibling* but only that it should signify *male-sibling*. The concept figures in the requirement simply as itself. We might represent the difference with "lines of coordination." For "male sibling" will signify a positively coordinated concept, in which there are lines of coordination from the concept itself to the two component concepts, where these lines of coordination are now taken to signify the relation of conjunction rather than identity. "Brother," on the other hand, will signify the negatively coordinated concept – the concept itself absent any positive line of coordination.[5]

Notes

Chapter 1

1 A large part of the present chapter was originally published in Fine (2003). I am grateful to the *Journal of Philosophy* for allowing me to reproduce the material.

2 I have stated the puzzle as a puzzle about variable types. There are corresponding versions of the puzzle for variable tokens and variable occurrences.

3 Cf. Dummett (1973, pp. 15–16). There is also the substitutional approach to quantification, which is subject to some of the same difficulties as the instantial approach and to some special difficulties of its own.

4 Bealer (1983) is the leading contemporary advocate of this approach. It is implicit in the so-called "algebraic semantics" for predicate logic.

5 Some hints at how a semantics of this sort might be developed are given in Fine (1989, pp. 237–8). I hope to deal more fully with the metaphysics and semantics of such abstraction elsewhere.

6 I might note, as a historical aside, that the views of Frege (1952) on the sense/reference distinction require that it be possible to provide an extensional semantics for the language of predicate logic, since he thought it should be possible to provide a compositional semantics at the level both of sense and of reference. The instantial approach is sometimes attributed to Frege (e.g., by Dummett, 1973, pp. 15–16). But it is only intelligible, at best, at the level of sense; and, for Frege, it is not even a viable option at the level of sense, since his views require that there should then be a *parallel* semantics at the level of reference. The Tarski semantics is also sometimes attributed to Frege. But this makes the semantic values typographic and so is neither satisfactory on its own account nor as an account of Frege's views. In the light of these considerations, it is hard to see how one can properly credit Frege with having a semantics for predicate logic.

7 Mathematicians sometimes use the strict equality sign "$\equiv$" in this way: "$x + y \equiv y + x$," for example, is used to indicate the universal truth of

"$x + y = y + x$." A similar difficulty arises for branching quantifiers, since the different "branches" of the quantifier do not occur in a set order, and we should note that it has often been supposed that ordinary language contains global quantification of this sort.

8   As with the notation for fractions or determinants: $\dfrac{x}{y}$ and $\dfrac{|xy|}{|uv|}$.

9   Some accounts of what a neutral relation might be are considered in Fine (2000a).

10 I have assumed that the quantified formula $\exists x A(x)$ contains no free variables. If it does, then we can only properly evaluate the formula by considering its connection to the free variables that it contains.

11 It has often been claimed that the telegraphic notation – with variables giving way to lines of coordination – provides a more perspicuous notation for predicate logic. The present approach can be seen as a way of making this notation precise and of providing it with a semantics. If logicians had taken the notation more seriously, instead of merely thinking of it as an informal device, then they would naturally have been led to the idea of a relational semantics.

12 It would also be of interest to develop a general framework for the study of relational syntax and semantics, of which the relational syntax and semantics for predicate logic could then be seen as a special case.

Chapter 2

1   Referentialists tend not to give these intuitions their due. A notable exception is Kaplan. In "Words" (Kaplan, 1990, p. 95, fn. 6), he writes, "I have come to think that two sentences whose syntax – perhaps here I should say, whose logical syntax – differs as much as 'a = a' differs from 'a = b' should never be regarded as having the same semantic value (expressing the same proposition), regardless of the semantic values of the individual lexical items 'a' and 'b'." But as far as I am aware, he gives no indication of how the difference in semantic value is to be achieved.

2   One might wonder whether we have two *identifiable* names (or uses of a name). For what justifies us in supposing that all of the tokens "on the left" and all of the tokens "on the right" are tokens of the very same name (or the same use)? The answer is simply that it is the speaker *taking* each subsequent token on the left or the right to have the same use as a previous token on the left or the right.

3   I myself have doubts as to whether this is an intelligible option for the consistent Fregean but, for present purposes, let us assume that it is.

4   Corefence between the names N and M may be defined *existentially* as $\exists x(\mathrm{Ref}(N, x) \ \& \ \mathrm{Ref}(M, x))$ or *universally* as $\forall x(\mathrm{Ref}(N, x) \equiv \mathrm{Ref}(M, x))$. The two definitions are equivalent given that N and M have unique referents, i.e. given $\exists!x\mathrm{Ref}(N, x) \ \& \ \exists!x\mathrm{Ref}(M, x)$. For now, I make this assump-

tion (and even assume it to be a semantic fact); and so the difference between the two definitions and the two corresponding definitions of strict coreference will not matter. However, when empty names are in question, it may be important to adopt the universal rather than the existential form of definition, since it will then be possible to distinguish between different empty names in regard to whether they strictly corefer.

5   Nathan Salmon has pointed out to me that there is some affinity between our notion of pure semantic fact and Carnap's notion of L-determinacy (Carnap, 1956, chapter II).

6   As a referee pointed out to me, even (i) might not be regarded as purely semantic if the truth of a sentence is taken to be consequential upon its expressing a true proposition.

7   I take the canonical formulation of semantic facthood to involve a sentence operator "it is a semantic fact that" (somewhat analogous to a modal operator). Thus we may say something like "it is semantic fact that 'Cicero' refers to Cicero"; and so no reference to a "fact" or "proposition" is strictly necessary. Although this is not a point I shall develop, I adopt a "thick" rather than a "thin" conception of a meaningful expression. Thus it will be built into the very identity of an expression such as "rot" that it belongs to the language it does and has the meaning that it does. There will therefore be at least two expressions spelt "rot," one for the English word and another for the German word; and there will be numerous names spelt "John."

8   Of course, this is not to deny that the language might evolve and that "Peter" might acquire an independent status as a name, just as in the second language.

9   To derive closure, we need only appeal to the quantificational version of the minimal modal logic, K. Nor does it help to use free logic in place of classical logic, since we do not want to be able to infer $K\exists x(Fx \& Gx)$ from $K(\exists y(x = y) \& Fx)$ and $K(\exists y(x = y) \& Gx)$ even though $\exists x(Fx \& Gx)$ is a free-logical consequence of $\exists y(x = y) \& Fx$ and $\exists y(x = y) \& Gx$.

10   The failure of our knowledge of singular propositions to be closed under classical consequence is generally recognized though, as far as I am aware, no attempt has been made either to isolate the notion of consequence under which such knowledge is closed or to investigate its properties.

11   We might also require that any object occurring in q' should occur in one of the premises $p_1', p_2', p_3', \ldots$ An analogous definition can be given for a relation of consequence between sentences or formulas. Note that the definition can be made to work whatever the base notion of consequence and also that we might allow some distinct occurrences of the same object to correspond to the same object under differentiation.

12   I have "straight" names in mind, of course – not something like "Superman," which might be thought to carry descriptive content.

13   The general theory of substitution, which I consider to be of great importance for both semantics and metaphysics, is briefly discussed in Fine (1989, 2000a).

14   Two variants on the notion of coordinated content should be mentioned though they will not be developed. First, one might allow the coordination-scheme $\mathcal{C}$ to relate occurrences of *distinct* individuals. This would correspond to the conflation of two individuals as one. Second, one might allow the uncoordinated contents $p_1, p_2, \ldots, p_n$ to contain occurrences of "blank" upon which the coordination-scheme $\mathcal{C}$ might then also be defined. Such contents would correspond to the use of empty names and would allow one to distinguish different empty names in terms of how they were coordinated.

The notion of manifest consequence may, of course, be explained in terms of coordination. Thus the inference from $p_1, p_2, \ldots, p_n$ to q will be manifestly valid if, for any coordination scheme $\mathcal{C}$ on $p_1, p_2, \ldots, p_n$, there is an extension of it to $p_1, p_2, \ldots, p_n, q$ under which the argument from $p_1, p_2, \ldots, p_n$ to q is valid (where validity for a coordinated inference is explained in terms of the validity of an inference in which each occurrence of an individual is replaced by its equivalence class under the coordination scheme).

15   It is a natural requirement on a sequences $p_1, p_2, \ldots, p_n$, when p_i and p_j are occurrences of the same proposition, that not *all* corresponding occurrences of individuals in p_i and p_j should be coordinated.

16   A loosely related version of the present puzzle is to be found in Dummett (1975). Note that, in contrast to the original Fregean puzzle, we do not need to appeal to any sentence containing the given names and nor do we make an implicit appeal to compositionality.

17   In stating the puzzle, there is no need to appeal to anything so strong as Transparency. Let us say that a fact concerning a given language is *accessible to semantic enquiry* if any rational, reflective and competent speaker of the language is in a position to know that the fact obtains on the basis of appropriate semantic investigation (this would exclude investigations into Roman history, say, or astronomy). Transparency may then be replaced by the assumption that semantic facts are accessible to semantic enquiry and Cognitive Datum by the assumption that the fact that "Cicero" and "Tully" corefer is not accessible to semantic enquiry.

18   Dummett writes, "it is an undeniable feature of the notion of meaning – obscure as that notion is – that meaning is *transparent* in the sense that, if someone attaches a meaning to each of two words, he must know whether these meanings are the same" (1978, p. 131; cf. 1973, p. 95). Perhaps he gives the formulation in terms of *sameness of meaning* rather than *meaning* because he thinks that the former notion is less obscure. But the formulation in terms of meaning is closer to what we think of as undeniable ("knowing what we mean"); and, if I am right, it is only this formulation that is correct.

19   Soames (1989) advances various arguments of this sort. However, I have not been able to find in his paper a telling argument against Transparency as it is stated here.

20 Actually, the various earlier arguments only require knowledge of particular semantic facts and so this second step in the defense of Transparency is not strictly required.

21 Some recent defenders of Transparency include Dummett (1993), Heck (1995), and Higgenbotham (1992). I make no attempt to compare these other formulations or defenses of the doctrine with my own.

Chapter 3

1 These difficulties are, of course, the analogue of difficulties that have been previously raised against the "algebraic" treatment of free variables (chapter 1, section E).

2 There may, of course, be consequential differences in what is believed. Thus the first person may believe that Cicero is a Roman orator while the second does not. But even these consequential differences will not in general be sufficient to distinguish between the coordinated content of what is believed.

3 It is not plausible to appeal to non-linguistic modes of presentation in the present context, since the hearer has no reason to suppose that the speaker will associate the same modes of presentation with the names as himself.

4 Here is the proof. Suppose that the thinker is justified in inferring that a has F & P & G & Q from I and the fact that a has F & P and a has G & Q, no matter what the purely qualitative properties P and Q might be (I assume that F and G do not involve the object a though they may involve other objects). Let Q be the negation ~P of P. Then from I, x's having F & P and x's having G & ~P, the thinker is justified in inferring that x has F & P & G &~P and hence is justified in inferring a contradiction ⊥, since the contradiction between P and ~P is manifest to him. Let F^e and G^e be the existential generalizations of F and G. Since the inference to ⊥ is *manifestly* valid, the thinker is justified in inferring ⊥ from I, $\exists x(F^e x \,\&\, Px)$ and $\exists x(G^e x \,\&\, \sim Px)$ and hence is justified in inferring ⊥ from I, $\exists x(F^e x \,\&\, G^e x \,\&\, Px)$ and $\exists x(F^e x \,\&\, G^e x \,\&\, \sim Px)$. But then the thinker is justified in inferring $\exists x(F^e x \,\&\, G^e x \,\&\, Px) \supset \forall x(F^e x \,\&\, G^e x \supset Px)$ and hence justified in inferring $\forall P[\exists x(F^e x \,\&\, G^e x \,\&\, Px) \supset \forall x(F^e x \,\&\, G^e x \supset Px)]$ from I, where P is a variable ranging over arbitrary purely qualitative properties. F^e & G^e is, therefore, the purely qualitatively property R that we are looking for. There is a related difficulty if we only allow the thinker to infer $\exists x(F^e x \,\&\, G^e x \,\&\, Px) \supset \forall x(F^e x \,\&\, G^e x \supset Px)$ for each *specific* purely qualitative property P.

5 Although this is not a topic I shall pursue, let me note that we may in a similar way provide an explanation of how it is a posteriori (though necessary) that Cicero is Tully. For what is a posteriori is the appropriately coordinated addition of the knowledge that Cicero is Tully to what one already knows. Thus what is properly said to be a posteriori is not the

proposition itself but the proposition in coordinative relation to some existing body of propositions. The Bayesian updating of credences can be taken care of in a similar way.

Chapter 4

1   For stylistic reasons, I will often use an indirect speech report when it would be more accurate to use a direct report.

2   The different versions of the puzzle and the relationships between them can be stated with some degree of rigor but this is not something that I shall attempt.

3   I switch from "believe" to "realize" to make the case more convincing.

4   This version of the puzzle appeals to "Strong Disquotation," but the principle is perhaps especially plausible in the case of first-person belief reports.

5   In addition to the weak and strict de dicto readings, there is the regular de dicto reading, which simply requires that the reporter speaker use the same names (as identified by their common use) as the reporter. It should be noted that these readings only concern the case of *positive* belief reports. I have not considered the special problems which arise when negative belief reports are allowed.

6   I take for granted that coordination is symmetric, though it is possible to dispense with this assumption.

7   An object might be taken to be *transparent* within a body of information if all of its occurrences are coordinated. This corresponds to assuming that the cognizer's "take" on the object should always be the same.

8   And, in general, it will imply that any two individual uses of the name are strictly coreferential.

9   The present considerations can be laid out within a formal framework (which is of some independent interest). The basic idea is that of a *manifold of names*. This is a triple $(I, N, >>)$, where I (individuals) is a non-empty set, N is a function taking each member i of I into a set N_i (the individual names belonging to i), and $>>$ (direct derivation) is a relation on $\cup_{i \in I} N_i$, subject to the following conditions:

1   the N_i for different $i \in I$ are disjoint;
2   for each $N \in N_i$ there is at most one M for which $N >> M$;
3   never $N >> M$ for N, M $\in N_i$; and
4   the converse of $>>$ is well-founded.

A manifold provides us with the supervenience base from which all questions of same-use etc. are to be settled.

Let us use $\approx$ for the relevant notion of same-use. Internal and External Link then correspond to the following two conditions:

(a)   Never N ≈ M for distinct N, M ∈ N_i; and

(b)   N >> M implies N ≈ M.

Thus a full solution to the puzzles should provide a definition of "≈" that is applicable to any manifold (i.e. to any possible puzzle case) and conforms to conditions (a) and (b). The need for a full solution – or even an account of what it might require – has not been generally appreciated.

Paul Hovda and an anonymous referee have pointed out that, under my proposed criterion for ≈, there might be an individual whose fractured use of a name spoils the possibilities of coordination for the rest of us. Perhaps we should soften the criterion by restricting the requirement of coherence to those individuals whose subjective states are in question. Thus instead of requiring that distinct individual uses M_i and M_j on the referential path M_1, M_2, . . . , M_k should not belong to the same individual, we need only require that they not belong to the same individual from a given subset J of I.

10   It was only because we ignored the possible relevance of coordination on "atomic" formulae such as Bel[A] in chapter 1 that we were there able to validate the principles of classical logic.

11   We should also note that the present semantics shows how it can be true that $\exists x \exists y(x = y \ \& \ \text{Bel}[x \neq y])$ even though it cannot be true that $\exists y\text{Bel}[y \neq y]$. For the latter requires a belief in the (positively) coordinated proposition that a given object is not identical to itself while the former only requires belief in the uncoordinated proposition. This example provides a simple illustration of how one cannot endorse the Substitutivity of Identicals under the present semantics, since $\forall x \forall y(x = y \supset (\text{Bel}[x \neq y] \supset \text{Bel}[y \neq y]))$ will not in general be true. The literalist semantics of Fine (1989, pp. 269–70), will also yield this result though it is not able to solve the earlier problem of making (1) and (2) compatible with the falsehood of (3).

12   Disquotation may fail for reports involving two or more uses of a name though it will, in general, hold for reports involving the single use of a name. But even here it may fail, as with the Peter-Petrov case above or when Peter reports himself as believing that Paderewski [according to his second use] is musical.

13   "Pointers" are often used to encode derivations in the implementation of automatic theorem-proving. If I am right, then pointers may not just be a convenience in this context but essential to the correct representation of logical form.

Postscript

1   The distinction between semantic requirements simpliciter and relative semantic requirements is analogous to the distinction I draw in Fine (1994) between necessity and essence.

2   Strictly speaking, we should also insist that the second expression occurs *as* an expression in the requirement and not just as an object that happens to be an expression. Thus we do not wish to take the phrase "the referent of 'Cicero'" to derive its reference from "Cicero," even though it is a semantic requirement on the phrase that it should be coreferential with "Cicero."

3   An analogous principle figures prominently in the logic of essence developed in Fine (2000b).

4   I have attempted to see mathematics as the product of stipulation (Fine, 2005b); and some of the ideas I use in developing an account of stipulation for mathematics may also be of relevance to the case of semantics. After all, both disciplines are "conservative" or neutral with respect to how things already are; and so it would not be surprising if there were a similar explanation of how they are capable of being conservative.

5   It might be thought that predicate terms should be taken to have application conditions rather than to signify concepts. It is not then altogether clear to me how the corresponding distinctions should be made out. Perhaps this is an argument for taking them to signify concepts.

References

Almog, J. (2006) "Is A Unified Treatment of Language-and-Thought Possible?," *Journal of Philosophy*, vol. CII, no. 10, pp. 493–531.

Almog, J., Perry, J., and Wettstein, H. (eds) (1989) *Themes from Kaplan*, Oxford: Oxford University Press.

Bealer, G. (1983) "Completeness in the Theory of Properties, Relations and Propositions," *Journal of Symbolic Logic*, vol. 48, no. 2, pp. 415–26.

Black, M. (1970) "The Identity of Indiscernibles," in M. Loux (ed.), *Universals and Particulars*, Garden City, NY: Doubleday, pp. 204–16.

Carnap, R. (1956) *Meaning and Necessity* (enlarged edn), Chicago: University of Chicago Press.

Davidson, D. (1967) "Truth and Meaning," *Synthese*, vol. XVII, pp. 304–23.

Dummett, M. (1973) *Frege: Philosophy of Language*, London: Duckworth, esp. ch. 2 and pp. 516–17.

Dummett, M. (1975) "Frege's Distinction between Sense and Reference," article 9 of *Truth and Other Enigmas*, Cambridge: MA: Harvard University Press, from "Frege", *Teorema*, vol. v., (1975), pp. 149–88.

Dummett, M. (1978) *Truth and Other Enigmas*, Cambridge: MA: Harvard University Press.

Dummett, M. (1993) "What Do I Know when I Know a Language," in *Seas of Language*, Oxford: Clarendon Press, pp. 94–105.

Fiengo, R. and May, R. (2005) *De Lingua Belief*, Cambridge: MIT Press.

Fine, K. (1985) *Reasoning with Arbitrary Objects*, Oxford: Blackwell.

Fine, K. (1989) "The Problem of De Re Modality," in Almog *et al.* (1989), pp. 197–272, reprinted in Fine (2005a).

Fine, K. (1994) "Essence and Modality," *Philosophical Perspective*, vol. 8, pp. 1–16; reprinted in P. Grim (ed.), *The Philosophers Annual for 1994*, volume 16, Stanford: CSLI.

Fine, K. (2000a) "Neutral Relations," *Philosophical Review*, vol. 109, no. 1, January, pp. 1–33.

Fine, K. (2000b) "Semantics for the Logic of Essence," *Journal of Philosophical Logic*, vol. 29, pp. 543–84.

Fine, K. (2003) "The Role of Variables," *Journal of Philosophy*, vol. 100, no. 12, pp. 605–31.

Fine, K. (2005a) *Modality and Tense: Philosophical Papers*, Oxford: Clarendon Press.

Fine, K. (2005b) "Our Knowledge of Mathematical Objects," in T. S. Gendler and J. Hawthorne (eds), *Oxford Studies in Epistemology*: vol. I, pp. 89–110, Oxford: Clarendon Press.

Frege, G. (1952) "On Sense and Reference," translation of "Über Sinn und Bedeutung," in P. T. Geach and M. Black (eds), *Translations from the Philosophical Writings of Gottlob Frege*. Oxford: Clarendon Press.

Heck, R. (1995) "The Sense of Communication," *Mind*, pp. 79–106.

Higgenbotham, J. (1992) "Belief and Logical Form," *Mind and Language*, vol. 6, pp. 244–69.

Kaplan, D. (1990) "Words," *Proceedings of the Aristotelian Society*, Supplementary vol. 64, pp. 93–119.

Kripke, S. (1979) "A Puzzle about Belief," in A. Margalit (ed.), *Meaning and Use*, Dordrecht: Reidel.

Kripke, S. (1980) *Naming and Necessity*, Cambridge, MA: Harvard University Press.

Lawlor, K. (2005) "Confused Thoughts and Modes of Presentation," *Philosophical Quarterly*, vol. 55, no. 218, pp. 137–48.

Lieb, H.-H. (1983) "Integrational Linguistics, vol. 1: General Outline", Amsterdam; Philadelphia: Benjamins (= *Current Issues in Linguistic Theory*, 17).

Mates, B. (1972) "Synonymity," L. Linsky (ed.), *Semantics and the Philosophy of Language*, Urbana: University of Illinois Press, pp. 111–38.

Putnam, H. (1954) "Synonymy and The Analysis of Belief Sentences," *Analysis*, vol. 14, pp. 114–22, reprinted in N. Salmon and S. Soames (eds), *Propositions and Attitudes*, (1989), Oxford: Oxford University Press, pp. 149–58.

Quine, W. V. O. (1952) *Methods of Logic*, London: Routledge and Kegan Paul.

Russell, B. (1903) *The Principles of Mathematics*, London: Allen & Unwin.

Salmon, N. (1992) "Reflections on Reflexivity," *Linguistics and Philosophy*, vol. 15, pp. 53–63.

Soames, S. (1989) "Semantics and Semantic Competence," *Philosophical Perspectives*, vol. 3, pp. 575–96.

Tarski, A. (1936) "Der Wahrheitsbegriff in den Formalisierten Sprachen", *Studia Philosophica I*, pp. 261–405, originally published in 1933, reprinted in *Logic, Semantics and Metamathematics*, Oxford, 1955.

Wittgenstein, L. (1922) *Tractatus-Logico-Philosophicus*, London: Routledge and Kegan Paul.

Index